OUTSPOKENLY YOURS,

OUTSPOKENLY YOURS,

COMMENTARIES: 1993-2016

Samuel Hazo

WORD ASSOCIATION PUBLISHERS
www.wordassociation.com
1.800.827.7903

Word Association Publishers
205 Fifth Avenue
Tarentum, Pennsylvania 15084
www.wordassociation.com
1.800.827.7903

ISBN: 978-1-63385-190-0

Library of Congress Control Number: 2017901702

Layout and Design by Jason Price

For John Hemington, John Allison and Greg Victor

CONTENTS

PREFACE

ALL BUT A FEW of these essays were originally published in the PITTSBURGH POST-GAZETTE. The remaining few appeared in the WASHINGTON REPORT and the NOTRE DAME MAGAZINE. All the essays are identified by date, but they are not all arranged chronically. I have simply placed some either individually or as a group where the essays had something thematically in common, even though written at different times. But I have not changed a word from the time of their first publication until now. If I repeat myself here and there, please overlook it. If I seem prescient in some or just plain wrong in others, then all I can say is that is how I thought at the time, and the responsibility for accuracy or error is entirely mine.

The majority of these essays reveal my reaction to and estimate of the nation we have become from the turn of the century until now. For me these first two decades have been the most disconcerting times in memory, exceeding even the tragedy of Vietnam, which should have been tragedy enough. The loss of life and treasure in the name of security has been unconscionable, and the political and social results and consequences will be with us for years, if not decades. I take no pleasure in saying this and would welcome being proved wrong, but some of the essays reflect this hue of pessimism, but never hopelessness.

I have always believed that the short essay or op. ed. is to the treatise what the short story is to the novel. The late James Reston of the NEW YORK TIMES once said that his writings as an editorialist made him think in three to five hundred word units. I now understand what he meant. But such limits imposed their own disciplines, and the writing was often the better for it. I can only hope that these essays achieve a similar result.

Samuel Hazo

1

A RIVERING CITY

PHOTOGRAPHED FROM THE STRATOSPHERE, the rivers of Pittsburgh (the Allegheny, the Monongahela and the Ohio) stand out like superscript or like the highlighted veins on a frontal drawing of a body chart. Uniting at a single point, they resemble an umbilicus that roots the city in its geography. And they also influence how it is perceived—not only by outsiders but by Pittsburghers themselves. To imagine Pittsburgh without its rivers would be similar to imagining Paris without the Seine, Rome without the Tiber, Florence without the Arno, London without the Thames, Dublin without the Liffey, or Germany and the Netherlands without the Rhine.

Unlike seas, rivers are companionable. Their strength is in their pulse and not in their breadth or depth. Without its rivers Pittsburgh would have no avenues for its boat traffic, none of its superb bridges, no docks or marinas, no convenient way to dispose of its treated sewage (an important but often overlooked consideration since water purification and the prevention of disease are crucial to public health) and no riverfronts.

Pittsburgh's riverfronts have evolved, it should be noted, from being wharves or mill sites into carefully graded shores where light industries, riverfront residences (quite expensive, by the way), corporate headquarters, parks, sports complexes and recreational, scientific and dining areas are now located. In brief, Pittsburgh without its rivers would be a city without a vortex and a natural geographic heartbeat. That vortex and that heartbeat create a magnetism that often keeps those who are here here or, if they've moved away, inclined to return. Some attribute this to the capacity of the city to engender a sense of at-homeness. This feeling of at-homeness seems to be a part of Pittsburgh manners and often manifests itself in totally unanticipated ways, as in the following. It so happened that a man was waiting impatiently in one of the concourses of the Pittsburgh International Airport. Apparently he was frowning. Suddenly a total stranger approached him, stood directly in front of him and said, "Smile, you're in Pittsburgh." The stranger turned and left, and the man who was frowning found himself smiling. I know the incident is true because I was the man with the frown.

If anyone is tempted to try this salutation on friend or stranger alike, the result will be inevitably the same. The salutee will invariably smile. A variant could now be "Smile, you're back in Pittsburgh." Many native Pittsburghers who left the city to find employment, adventure or diversion elsewhere or who retired to warmer climates have quietly moved back. It seems to alter an old maxim that you can get Pittsburghers out of their city, but you can't get their city out of them. A certain civic allegiance was deep-rooted in these returnees and made them look homeward when they were away so that in time they responded to this impulse and came back to their origins. Often they even returned to their original neighborhoods.

The notion of neighborhoods is engrained in Pittsburgh life. Inner city areas like the South Side have retained their identities, as have boroughs like Aliquippa. Aliquippa was once a thriving community of steelworkers. With the demise of the steel industry the economy of the borough predictably worsened. Take a tour of the business district of Aliquippa today, and you will find numerous boarded-up storefronts and other evidence of closure. But Aliquippa's residential neighborhoods still show an ancestral and careful attention of lawns, house maintenance and, for lack of a better word, appearances. Go to other neighborhoods like Polish Hill, Lawrenceville, Troy Hill or even the rivertowns (Monessen, for example), and you will also find them clean though wounded. I suppose it all comes down to neighborhood pride. A few years ago a campaign was launched by certain civic promoters to make Pittsburgh more attractive to tourists. One woman, who had had her fill of what she considered an ill-conceived form of outreach, wrote a letter-to-the-editor in which she stated shamelessly that "Pittsburgh is not a city for tourists but for residents." And for her that was that. But the nationally known writer and essayist Brendan Gill, after insinuating that Pittsburgh was one of the most beautiful cities in the world, went a step further and took an outsider's liberty of paying Pittsburgh the ultimate compliment, "If Pittsburgh were situated somewhere in the heart of Europe, tourists would eagerly journey hundreds of miles out of their way to see it."

I am a Pittsburgher by birth and choice. The only times I have been away from the city for extended periods were when I attended the University of Notre Dame in the late forties and then served on active duty in the United States Marine Corps in the early fifties. As a resident I have made it my business to become familiar with the city's past and present, beginning with the Pittsburgh-related events of the French and Indian War (Fort Pitt at the fusing of the Monongahela and Allegheny was originally named Fort Duquesne after the Marquis before the British honored William Pitt with the title), the battles of the Revolutionary War, the social transformation caused by the Industrial Revolution and the attraction the city had for immigrants hungry for employment and a new life in the early decades of the twentieth century. The relics of each period are omnipresent. General Braddock is buried east of Uniontown where the French and Indians defeated him, and Washington's Fort Necessity still stands less than an hour's drive from Pittsburgh. It has always seemed ironically significant that Uniontown is the birthplace of George Catlett Marshall, who was Eisenhower's superior in World War II before he became President Truman's Secretary of State and was the architect of the Marshall Plan that decisively saved Europe after the war. I don't know why Marshall's name is part of this revolutionary pantheon for me, but it could be that he, like Washington, was a general for the working day and then became a visionary and statesman afterward. The parallel exists.

My attitude toward Pittsburgh is a mixture of hard historical facts, bits of sociology, sentiment and a living sense of the past that in part defines the present. During the worst of the foreboding days of the Cold War, all of these strains fused in a poem of mine entitled "Pittsburgh in Passing":

> Between old battles and the ones I should
> be seeing, I have lost my circus eyes.
> Birthdays are deathdays. I feel the glaciering
> of centuries beneath the pulse of clocks
> and through the blown-out candles of my blood.
>
> I stand unarmed where Braddock's armies stood.
> Instead of Hurons I see acres piped
> and sewered for our waste and mined with bones
> of Quakers, Indians and immigrants.
> Three decades in the woods of William Penn
>
> have left me kin to all the buried men
> who claimed this wilderness and named this town.
> Where Washington marched in buckskin, I can drive
> through battlefields of signs and ironworks,
> inhale unrevolutionary air
>
> and damn the siren waking me to war-
> alerts each Monday of the year. Senates
> have bolstered us with bunkercaves and rockets.
> A palisade of missiles rings the town
> while banking and burlesque thrive back to back
>
> in the same building. Threats of surprise attack
> would bench a naked tease and the most correct
> of tellers flank to flank in a joint shelter.
> No one objects. Shielded around the clock
> by minutemen in radar shacks, we tomb

the Hiroshima world beside old Rome
and older Troy while mayors fatten us
with talk. No one admits we walk on skulls,
no one prays Isaiah back to speak
the truth without refining it to please.

The siren spins. The aborigines
and whites who battled here are six wars old.
Chained to a different blunderbuss, we sleep
in cemeteries screened by warhead forts
and dream our moats are still the seven seas.

While recognizing the allegiance of native Pittsburghers to the city, most residents admit with regret that the city's core population has shrunk and is still shrinking. People have moved to the suburbs or have moved away completely. Many young people cannot find jobs that are commensurate with their talents and skills and subsequently re-locate. The result is that the population of the city proper, i.e., those individuals and families that make up the tax base, has declined from more than 600,000 in the middle of the last century to less than 400,000 now. The departure of the young has created almost by default a population of senior citizens. On average, Pittsburgh has the second oldest population of any city in the United States.

But one thing a city cannot do is re-locate. Detroit, on the contrary, has seen its inner city population move outward beyond its eight and ten-mile limits. The reasons were, to be frank, both racial and economic. Before the businesses and shopping centers followed this exodus, those who left pursued a well-known pattern common to many in and around New York. They lived, bred and slept in the suburbs and came to the city to work. In due course Detroit's industries moved after the departed so that some parts of the city from the Renaissance Center outward were uninhabited. The entire city in effect slid toward Flint. One of the reasons this is not possible for Pittsburgh is that it is positioned like the hub of a wheel. The downtown area is literally locked into itself by its very geography and, of course, by the rivers. In this regard Pittsburghers take a special pride in pointing out as an aside that the Monongahela and Allegheny rivers at their juncture actually create the Ohio. Such explanations satisfied everyone to whom I have mentioned this except for one French tourist. A true Cartesian, he frowned and responded: "In my country when one river meet another river, it only mean that one river just stop and the other river keep going." Such dissents are not common, but I suppose there is something always to be said for listening to the French inclination toward nuance that frequently changes customary perceptions.

Having been built at the vortex of three rivers (two if the French version is accepted), Pittsburgh has the rhythm of rivers in its very personality. Unlike seas and oceans, which are like nouns in their stationery size and presence, rivers are more like verbs. They are destined by their very natures to flow or die. When I drive alongside the Allegheny or the Monongahela or the Ohio, I feel the difference between car-time and river-time. The rivers pump on like blood at a specific speed and tempo in their channeled courses. If dredged, the river bottoms would yield everything from sunken barges (and strangely one Air Force bomber still unrecovered) to coffee cans, coins, miscellaneous junk and human bones. Once used exclusively for purposes related to the steel and coal industries, the rivers now accommodate sternwheelers as tourist attractions or floating sites for private and corporate parties. Motor boats are part of river traffic now, occasionally towing water skiers. Varsity rowing and sculling teams come and go.

If you watch a river from one of its banks, you almost comprehend what the mystery of time and history is supposed to mean. But rivers have posed a more prosaic challenge to bridge-builders, and the builders have responded accordingly. There are more than eight hundred bridges in the city and more than twenty-one hundred in Allegheny County—a national record, by the way. Many of them were designed by some of the most distinguished bridge-architects in the world, i.e., Roebling and Lindenthal, to name but two. Viewed from a bridge a river seems to draw you into itself, and you feel an atavistic fear that is akin to the fear that many feel when they look down at the sidewalk from the top floor of a skyscraper or when they peer into the eye of a volcano from an overpassing plane or even when they stare into the dark at the bottom of a well. But when a river is observed from the safe sea-level perch of a riverbank, it almost defines what freedom is in its pristine state or what natural force means. If what Heraklitos wrote is true, namely, that no man can step into the same river twice (because he is not the same man, and it is not the same river), then it's possible to conclude that the river symbolized for him—as it did for Mark Twain, Hart Crane and Thomas Wolfe—time itself. It mocks those miniscule toys we tell time with on our wrists or in cars or on the walls and mantels of our homes. The river seems to tell time as time measures itself.

And a city that has a confluence of rivers in its very anatomy is constantly reminded of that whether it wants to be reminded or not. Even as the shape of the city changes—new roads, new or transformed neighborhoods, new plans for regeneration (both laudatory, as in the case of the gentrification of the downtown area with apartment buildings and condos where defunct stores used to be, or questionable in the extreme, as with the construction of a gambling casino on the North Side as a way to bring revenue to the city a la Las Vegas), the river, in the words of Oscar Hammerstein, "just keeps rollin' along." In a poem of mine called "Signs of Life in a Sundown City" I subconsciously wrote of the contrast without realizing what I had done until I completed the poem. In many ways the poem tells me without pulling a punch what I think the city has become and is becoming.

> We number less than half of what
>   we were four decades back.
> The young look elsewhere for their lives.
> The old grow older and die.
> Mansions of a long dead gentry
>   calcify like skulls.
>   Museums
>   lease from millionaires what artists
>   painted while they starved.
>   On streets
>   that once were prime, the smell
>   of oligarchy gone bourgeois is palpable.
> The current synonym for blackjack,
>   poker, craps and slots
>   is gaming.

Uptown at midnight
the currency is drugs and guns,
and murderers grow younger
by the day.
Regardless, the trees
parade in place at permanent
attention.
Simply by happening,
each day proclaims itself unique
and unrepeatable.
And two
undaunted rivers fork and fuse
into a third that flows into a fourth
that steers in silence to the sea
that's stayed the same since Genesis.

Culturally speaking, Pittsburgh offers a generous welcome to all the arts. and the city's philanthropic institutions as well as its leading commercial institutions are forthcoming in their support. This includes diverse theater groups, a first class symphony, an opera company, several dance companies, several university presses (two of which, Pitt's and Carnegie Mellon's, publish nationally recognized and awarded poets whose books are distributed wherever books of poetry are sold), choral societies, an international forum for American and foreign poets and an art collection in the Carnegie Institute that can hold its own with any. Like many American cities it has lost all but one of its major newspapers. That one plus one other are trying to fill the void. In the face of competition with the internet, radio and television, the continued existence of print journalism is as much under threat in Pittsburgh as it is elsewhere in the country, and this is regrettable. Recognition may come from seeing or hearing the news, but understanding only comes from language, and it is there that the written (or printed) word is supreme.

For many years Pittsburgh was considered provincial by outsiders who came to live here as a result of company transfers and the like. I have always considered this pure snobbery. Pride in place and provincialism have never been synonymous. Those who have called Pittsburgh provincial seem to have little understanding how local pride is earned here. It's earned by "stayers" who contribute to the daily life of the city within the limits of their ability and their influence. Transients who have come and attempted to re-make the city in their own image have eventually been shunted to the peripheries by the centrifugal forces of urban life itself. But the civic pride that is generated by the habitual efforts of the "stayers" is an expanding and not a restricting force. It is the very enemy of provincialism, which is usually interpreted to apply to those who refuse to see or become involved in what is beyond their immediate milieu. Such an atavistic provincialism seems to me virtually impossible now in light of new presences that have emerged in Pittsburgh's social, cultural and industrial life.

The most obvious social example is the presence of new immigrants. These foreign nationals (or rather ex-nationals) have increased exponentially from the 1950's onward. Today they are so evident that their existence has become commonplace, not only among university students but in the professional classes as well, particularly in medicine and industry. You can hear numerous foreign languages spoken openly where formerly they were spoken only in residences. Restaurants now cater to a myriad of tastes, and each cuisine has its devoted clientele: Northern Italian, Spanish, Middle Eastern, German, Indian, Chinese, Irish, Cambodian, Vietnamese, Japanese, Jewish, Peruvian, Taiwanese, French and Calabrian.

A large influx of doctors from the Orient and the Middle East is today an established constituency, not only in the world-famous UPMC (University of Pittsburgh Medical Center made famous by being the place where Dr. Jonas Salk created the polio vaccine and where Dr. Thomas Starzl pioneered heart and kidney transplant surgery) but in private practice as well. And the city's colleges and universities have a bounty of students as well as faculty members of foreign birth on their campuses. Such internationality is not surprising since American higher education has long had a magnetic pull on students and scholars from abroad. Intensive recruiting programs for both students and faculty will continue to keep this trend alive, but many administrators have been advised not to forget where the reputations of their institutions were forged and what made them what they are. The answer is and will invariably be that the major portion of students will continue to be home-grown. Duquesne University, where I taught for many years, has for generations educated the city's pharmacists, lawyers, judges, primary and secondary school teachers as well as its music instructors and band leaders. Many believe this legacy has far more historical significance than having students from 104 countries now represented on its campus. On the other hand such international diversity demonstrates that the reputation of America's universities transcends our country's borders. This is certainly true of Pittsburgh's major universities and its community college (Pitt, Duquesne, Carnegie-Mellon, Chatham, Carlow, La Roche, Robert Morris, Point Park and Allegheny Country Community College.) Local students form the core of the student bodies, but all these institutions accommodate a steadily enlarging international population.

Further confirmation of Pittsburgh's cosmopolitanism is the number of industries in the city (and Allegheny County) that are foreign-owned. Currently there are more than 150 industries that so qualify. Of these, 62 are German-owned, 27 British, 14 Canadian, 12 Japanese and sundry others whose owners are Australian, Austrian, Belgian, Brazilian, Czechoslovakian, Danish, Finnish, French, Indian, Israeli, Italian, Korean, Dutch, Norwegian, Swedish and Swiss. These industries deal in everything from mining machinery and metal products to glass containers, cement, locks, chemicals, alloys, optical equipment, wood veneer, stainless steel, cookies, printing presses, plastics, pharmaceuticals, television sets, windows, window shades, ceramics and office furniture. Any Pittsburgher or anyone else who might be inclined to think of the city as isolationist or provincial in economic terms need only to look around to be disabused of the illusion.

Everyone who knows Pittsburgh well will concede without much hesitation that it is in essence a city for workers. Whether motivated by the Protestant work-ethic or the simple urgency to survive (something that the immigrants of the last century and since have left as their legacy) or the desire of the most recent generations to "make it" or the simple and sacred desire of men and women to do a "good job," the reliance upon work as a dominant force in social life is a given. It is not by accident that the tradition of trade unionism was nurtured here by Philip Murray, David MacDonald and others. Nor has it been by accident that many of those who became prosperous here (as opposed to others of more recent vintage) more often than not returned a good portion of their wealth to the city where they earned it. The names of Carnegie, Mellon and Heinz come to mind as the most prominent. Free libraries throughout the area were created at the flinty and dogged insistence of Andrew Carnegie, albeit with the proviso that the name of Carnegie should appear on every one. Paul Mellon's munificence always included Pittsburgh even though projects like the National Gallery and the Bollingen project at Princeton deservedly received more extensive support. And the foundations of the Heinz family, whether under company auspices or separately, have supported and continue to support cultural and educational life in multiple ways.

This tradition of work may explain public resistance to the introduction of casino gambling to Pittsburgh. Initially the sponsors of this idea used the more euphemistic word "gaming" to make gambling more palatable to the public. One advocate even strove to purify the idea further by stating that there was not a word against gambling in the Bible. He simply saw it as wholesome adult entertainment for those who could afford it. Despite being told that the casino would provide hundreds of jobs and that the city would derive revenue from casino profits, which would offset to some extent the money it was not getting from its shrinking tax base, the public initially rejected the idea out of hand, and the state legislature subsequently tabled the issue on constitutional grounds. The pro-gambling lobby did not relent. They knew that the desire to make money through chance had a strong appeal, and they persisted until a franchise was awarded, permitting the construction of a casino near the Point (the juncture of the Allegheny and Monongahela).

Whether the subject is gambling or promotion tourism, it is obvious to amateur and professional alike that making money is the basic motivation. The assumption is that whatever brings money into the city is beneficial. The same argument has been made for years vis-à-vis the baseball, football and hockey franchises. But here it seems more legitimate because sports, despite the recent scandals with drugs and the like, are somehow linked to civic pride and civic allegiance. David L. Lawrence, perhaps Pittsburgh's greatest mayor, was adamant until his death that he never wanted Pittsburgh to become a minor league city, and every city official since has shared this conviction and vision. And the public at large has the same disposition. No one disputes that there would be a loss in the city's status nationally if the Steelers, Pirates or Penguins would up and leave.

But what of the arts? And what of arts organizations, which are by law non-profit? There is no question that different criteria apply here, but there is disagreement on what these criteria should be. One of the basic truths of all non-for-profit organizations is that they survive through the largesse and generosity (deductibly or otherwise) of their corporate, private or individual supporters. Their tenuous mission is to be faithful to the art they offer while losing money as slowly and wisely as possible.

How are their existences justified or justifiable when measured against the merciless perceptions of bottom-line thinkers?

One form of justification is to claim that the various arts and arts organizations (of which there were 69 at last count, beginning with the Afro-American Music Institute and concluding alphabetically with The Upstairs Theater and the Y Music Society) generate an economic benefit to Allegheny County in the amount of $368,000,000 per annum. In addition, these organizations have an annual business impact on Pittsburgh itself in the range of $251,000,000. Add to this approximately $1,100,000 in hotel revenues on a yearly basis. Totaled, these are not negligible figures, and those who are persuaded by figures alone take them quite seriously. But is this the whole story? Do they really focus on the human importance of the arts to Pittsburgh's (or any city's) social life? If the arts did not bring in a single dime to the city's coffers and to the wallets of businessmen, would they still be indispensable to civic life? If history is to be believed, the answer is an absolute yes.

The visionary dynamism of the arts inevitably speaks to human beings in their complete personalities. One listens to music (not Musak) with one's total self as one reads a novel or a poem or sees deeply into a painting or a sculpture or is empathetically drawn into the action of a drama. Few things other than the arts do this. Entertainment does not and cannot do it whether it be a situation comedy, a routine of a comedian with a microphone, a football or baseball game or, regrettably, the news presented as entertainment. Add to this those social forces that speak to us only in partial terms—as consumers, voters, customers, retirees, travelers and so on—, and you conclude that human beings in their entirety are not being addressed.

And numerous forms of automation contribute further to the ongoing dumbing down of private manners in public life. Who has not had the experience of telephoning a company or agency and been told by a neutered voice that "Your call is important to us" and then been kept waiting indefinitely for the "importance" to be recognized by some technician in India or the Philippines? And the custom proliferates. It becomes more and more difficult to get the attention of a single human being. The arts stand opposed to all that. They speak to the individual first and foremost, and they speak without falsity or purpose of evasion from our most intimate impulses. One of the best explanations of art's staying power and why its originality cannot be gainsaid was given by E. M. Forster: "The work of art is the only material object in the universe which may possess internal harmony. All the others have been pressed into shape from outside, and when the mould is removed they collapse. The work of art stands by itself, and nothing else does. It achieves something which has always been promised by society, but always delusively."

Pittsburgh's history during the last fifty years could be an exemplar for America as a whole. The alliance of Pittsburgh philanthropy and the arts asserted itself persistently during that era, and many organizations and individuals in the private sector rallied to fill the void that the National Endowment for the Arts could not fill for political as well as economic reasons. Indeed they did so even though they openly acknowledged that their support could not be sustained indefinitely without government assistance. Just in a single year before the turn of the century the city and county funded thirty-one not-for-profit organizations for a total of $222,361, and the Allegheny

Regional Asset District (ARAD), which derives its budget from sales taxes in Allegheny County, distributed grants to eighty-eight not-for-profit organizations during the same period for a total of $64,755,500 of which $59,338,500 went to arts organizations. The fact that the city and the county did not ally themselves with atavistic forces that regard the arts as merely ornamental struck many as a kind of landmark in the history of Pittsburgh. And why not? Enlightened cultures from the Age of Pericles to the Florence of the Medicis have realized that support of the arts, regardless of controversy or friction, is an act of munificence that enhances a society by encouraging visions that the arts alone are able to provide to its citizenry. Perhaps this partly explains why Pittsburgh has become the permanent residence of writers in all genres—poets, novelists, essayists, historians, science fiction authors and playwrights.

Despite the worrisome decline in its population and the adoption of questionable methods to compensate for its diminishing tax base, Pittsburgh has a population that has demonstrated a capacity to try to solve its own problems. The Pittsburgh Renaissance that rid the city of smog was but one of its signal accomplishments. The current plans to gentrify the downtown area seems a sensible answer to the gaps left by commercial markets that have been unable to compete with the proliferation of shopping malls in the suburbs (with free parking) and been forced to close. The fact that the usable gates at the Pittsburgh International Airport have been cut almost in half, whether attributed to the decline in air travel since September 11, 2001 or to the lack of vision of participating airlines, particularly US Airways, is a serious loss for a facility (designed by local architect Tasso Katelas) that has been identified as the number one airport in the United States and the third most beautiful and efficient airport in the world. And, like many American cities, the problems of traffic, aging infrastructure, drug-related crime and the regrettable cheapening of social life for reasons too numerous to list are all in need to attention, but there are individuals and groups that are determined to attend to and solve them.

At this point I could refer again to the city's rivers as well as its three intra-city parks (Schenley, Highland and Frick) to suggest how nature and a respect for nature would be symbolic allies in our quest for regeneration. They simply go on being their best and only possible themselves. But there was an event that happened less than a decade ago that demonstrated conclusively for me that a city is as much a home as an actual home is to its inhabitants. On the morning of September 11, 2001, I had already left for work and did not know of the havoc and devastation that had been visited on New York, Washington and a field near Somerset, Pennsylvania. A few hours later I closed my office and came home. My wife told me that she had gone into our yard shortly after I left and looked up to see a large, low-flying jet pass overhead and continue east. Whether it was the very jet that was forced down after its passengers attempted to overpower its highjackers, I don't know and will never know. But it certainly could have been. My wife then went back into the house where she watched the day's events unfold on television. She stayed there, not merely to watch television but because being home was the only place she wanted to be. When I closed my office (as did thousands of others in the city) and came home, it seemed to me that home was the only place left to go. As a reaction to the catastrophes that had been visited on the nation, we all yielded to an atavistic desire to be with those dearest to us in a space we called our own. In a poem of mine called "September 11, 2001," I strove to put this feeling into the only words that came to me at that time.

The hawk seems almost napping
in his glide.
His arcs are perfect
as geometry.
His eyes hunger
for something about to panic,
something small and unaware.
Higher by six thousand feet
an airbus vectors for its port,
its winglights aiming dead
ahead like eyesight.
The natural
and scheduled worlds keep happening
according to their rules…
"We interrupt
this program…"
Inch by inch
the interruption overrules both worlds,
engulfing us like dustfall
from a building in collapse.
The day
turns dark as an eclipse.
We head
for home as it to be assured
that home is where we left it.

The impulse to come home to be assured "that home is where we left it" is probably the same impulse that keeps Pittsburghers in Pittsburgh and beckons original Pittsburghers back. These people both are and perpetuate the city in their lives, visions and deeds and possess the capacity to re-create it. Pittsburgh, which has been a national forerunner among cities in its capacity to re-create itself environmentally, industrially, artistically and philanthropically, has shown and is showing that its energies for change are far from atrophied. Though Pittsburghers are somewhat conservative in the "We have to think things through before we decide what to do" sense, they by and large have the familial, neighborhood and civic stamina to avoid the sterility of mere nostalgia or its equally vain counterpart—escape into a false dream of the future. The rivers are always there to remind them that basically life is always differently the same, that our common address is the present tense and that our sense of our own mortality is our common starting point. The man who said, "Smile, you're in Pittsburgh," was in a sense saluting not me alone but his fellow man by welcoming me to the present moment, even though he may not have realized it. And that's as good a place to start as any.

2008

2

FATTENING THE FEW

DURING THE REAGAN AND BUSH PRESIDENCIES there seemed to be two Americas. There was a vision of America that existed in the White House. And then there was the America that existed. The gap between the two became wider and wider – the world of ideology vs. the world of fact.

Since facts do not change to accommodate ideology and since ideology cannot change without betraying itself, we witnessed the politics of blame and diversion. There were endless put-downs of Jimmy Carter. There were wearying excoriations of tax-tax-tax and spend-spend-spend members of the "other party" by those who would become the biggest spenders-spenders-spenders in our history-history-history.

We are now uncomfortably aware, as Sen. Ernest Hollings, D-S.C., has stated, that a selective type of yuppie prosperity was built on a foundation of three trillion (the increase in the national debt from 1980 to 1992) in bad checks. We also know absolutely that we had administrations that seemed committed to circumventing (allowing for "plausible deniability") the accepted safeguards of representative government – from the end runs of Colonel Oliver North and Admiral John Poindexter to George Bush's pronouncement that he would go to war in the Persian Gulf if he had congressional approval or not.

We see now that the fattening of the few was accompanied by indifference to, or disregard of, the many who had the misfortune to be unfortunate. We see what deregulation has done to the airline industry, for example, with the resultant increase in the cost of domestic travel. We saw and see that the burden placed upon local and state governments when federal assistance dried up after taxes were "reduced across the board" was more than they could bear. We also see that the S&L debt, which was passed on to the (us) government when uninsured investments turned sour, will continue to be paid into the indefinite future, as Secretary of the Treasury Lloyd Bentsen and President Clinton have recently affirmed. And we see that the Pyrrhic military victories over self-created enemies are not the final solutions or new orders they were supposed to be.

When governments strive to act outside the law and even outside of history, the law of compensation intervenes. Reality begins to ask its due. We can conclude now that government of and for the few was not a democracy but an oligarchy. Oligarchic governments have always regarded the people as their enemy – sums of population to be ruled, not governed. The inevitable result is that distrust gradually replaces trust on both sides, and the breakdown in the social contract between the elected and the electorate begins at that moment.

Since a democracy is sustained by trust (and by trust alone regardless of the wheeling and dealing done in its name), the breakdown in trust left us with the problems that distrust creates. This goes beyond scapegoating the two presidents who sought to persuade us that reality was illusion and vice-versa (although it is difficult to absolve two independently wealthy men who left us and our children and possibly their children a gargantuan debt as their common legacy).

But scapegoating will not do away with fears for personal safety in neighborhoods, work areas, schools and, lately, automobiles. It will not renew faith in those activities (art and education) that are the natural enemies of hypocrisy. It will not stop the splitting of the electorate along racial, ethnic or sexual lines. It will not keep justice from being mocked while the guilty with the right connections are quietly pardoned. It will not keep vindictiveness at the highest level from being a respected part of political discourse (Newt Gingrich is but the latest incarnation of this Agnew-inspired tradition).

Those who have seen through this public-relations fandango from the start are now beginning to write the books that describe the damage done to the country by the profit-firsters, the corporate raiders, the inside-traders and their like. (I recommend Sen. Eugene J. McCarthy's "A Colony of the World" and George F. Kennan's "Around the Cragged Hill" as starters). Such writings will not please the Reagan warriors, the new world orderers or the Buchananites. They will go on attacking the legacy of John F. Kennedy, the National Endowment for the Arts, the United Nations, Social Security and the civil rights movement, to name only a few of their favorite targets. They will never admit that capitalism is, after all, just a system. It is not a complete view of man, any more than Marxism was.

Unrestrained, it operates under the naked imperatives of initiative and greed. The true believers in such a limited view of the nature of man believe that government should provide for the national defense and then get out of the way.

Apparently, they never bothered to read the preamble to the Constitution which states that the role of government is not only to "provide for the common defense" but also "to promote the general welfare and secure the blessings of liberty for ourselves and our posterity."

The ultimate basis for such a constitutional and participatory adventure in government is trust. Loss of trust is the mortal wound beside which all other hurts are venial. Unlike a broken arm, it does not heal stronger at the break. Usually it does not heal at all. This is because trust is a quality that exists in its totality, or it does not exist at all. It does not almost exist – not in government, in the relation of doctor and patient, teacher and student, friend and friend, or husband and wife. What John Donne said of the trust of mutual love and its concomitant loss is as true for a democracy as it is for those who know the high noon of reciprocal faith and affection:

> Love is a growing, or full constant light;
> And his first minute, after noon, is night.

The implication of this statement for people in a free society is obvious, primary and inescapable. In us we must trust.

1993-2004

3

TO TEACH, PERCHANCE TO LEARN

A SKI INSTRUCTOR ONCE TOLD ME, "Anyone who teaches anybody anything is doing God's work." Having always regarded teaching as a vocation and not simply a job, I agreed. Whether the subject is skiing or literature is not the issue; what matters is that the knowledge is freely shared. If all we have in this life is what we can give away, what profession offers a better conduit for such giving (exclusive, of course, of parentage) than teaching?

Since what we don't know always exceeds what we do know, every teacher – an elder student among younger ones – has the opportunity to share not only his knowledge but also his ignorance with students who do just the same. Neither is penalized for the sharing, and both emerge the richer for it.

At a time when education is often lip-served while being philosophically and financially undermined, when teachers are gratuitously told that they are the only ones in this world who do not have the right to strike, when some colleges and universities often sell out their curricula on the principle that the student, like the customer, is always right, when the tentacles of trendy sociology, ideology and the need for gun control among juveniles have tended to distract us from the pivotal importance of education in the life of the nation, it's not a waste of time to cite a few fundamental facts.

The first and most obvious is that most Americans spend roughly a third of their lives in school. The second, which is equally obvious and unavoidable, is that we all spend a third of our lives sleeping. The remaining third is devoted to what we habitually call "our lives."

Education, therefore, deserves to be seen for what it is – not simply as a time of preparation to "get through," but as a definite time of life. Like childhood or adolescence, it is what it is before it is anything else. The intellectual life and the pursuit of truth are ends in themselves, and education is concerned with both. It is a time when students can learn the "skills of being" that are the core of the intellectual life and can become habituated to the pursuit of truth as central to their lives then and thereafter. Teachers are the stewards in this slow, invaluable process.

Good teachers are as rare as saints or heroes. Today in many high schools and colleges they must be not only good but also brave. First they must fight the false gods of learning – phonics instead of spelling, adjustment instead of excellence, indulgence instead of discipline. Then they often find themselves in physical jeopardy in places where no such jeopardy should exist – in their very classrooms. It is to the everlasting credit of their faith and idealism that people still want to be teachers. Money is certainly not a primary inducement.

In this regard it is difficult to understand why the public is often against teachers who strike to achieve a salary level and associated benefits in their later years that certain lawyers, engineers and hospital specialists receive as starting salaries. It is doubly ironic to learn that those most opposed to these just demands are those whose affluence is often traceable, not to luck or inheritance, but to their own education by these very teachers or their predecessors.

Almost everyone has had the experience of having had his or her life influenced permanently by one or two inspiring teachers.

Students held John Henry Newman in such esteem at Oxford that they simply said, "Credo in Newmanum" ("I believe in Newman") when queried about their personal philosophies. In our own era one thinks of Mark Van Doren, Mortimer Adler, Dr. Robert Woodward, Sister Maura Eichner, Gilbert Highet and Page Smith. The great administrators of the era have also been tireless educators, teaching courses even as they administered: Woodrow Wilson of Princeton, Jacob Klein of St. John's, Robert Maynard Hutchins of Chicago, A. Whitney Griswold and A. Bartlett Giamatti of Yale.

I can never forget two teachers at my own alma mater, Notre Dame. One was Gilford Burdick, the swimming instructor and coach. He taught non-swimmers to swim, and he made ordinary swimmers into master swimmers. Over 40 years how much confidence did he instill, how many champions did he groom? Above all, how many lives did he save?

The second was Frank O'Malley. A teacher of literature, he had the gift of inspiring students to do better than their best. Of course, he could be acerbic. If you forgot your text or your notebook, he would say crisply, "Why didn't you forget your lungs?" But he corrected papers promptly and brilliantly, and he never missed a class. And his scholarly essays were as well-wrought as poems.

When he died, he was laid in state in front of his classroom. After the funeral, his family and friends went to his bachelor's room on campus to look for "the big book" he had been rumored to be working on. Instead they found on one side of his bed all the books his former students had published (Edwin O'Connor dedicated THE LAST HURRAH to him). On the other side of the bed were the best papers his students had written over five decades. And under the bed was a shoe box filled with uncashed checks – repayments that students had sent to him for "loans" he had made to them when they needed the money.

Stories and profiles of teachers like these are in everybody's memory. Recognized or not, rewarded financially or not, these men and women are the defenders of what should become our country. When asked what America stands for, we do not talk about insider trading, chicanery in public life, greed in the marketplace, gangs and drive-by shootings, the prolonged juvenilia of many professional athletes or even what is called the two-party system. We talk ultimately about those values that are fostered in public and private education.

Teachers are the ones who do that fostering. Those who think that this fostering is not primarily important and worthy of sacrifice and support need only imagine what the country would be like without it.

1994

4

THE HABIT OF COURAGE

EVERYONE ADMIRES A HERO, and we all think we know the hero when we see one. But do we?

Historically there has always been an association of heroism with courage, usually though not always physical courage. But what is courage? Aristotle defined it simply as the quality that enables us to do what is right – habitually. A courageous man or woman for Aristotle was someone who did the right thing – not once or twice – but on a regular basis, regardless of opposition or consequence.

If we accept this as true, then it relegates to the levels of bravado, daring or mere spontaneity what we mistakenly identify as heroic or courageous acts. Evel Knievel's motorcycle-leap over ten parked cars, a free fall from 10,000 feet, a bungee jump, the scaling of a Himalayan peak or something like Rocky Balboa's stubborn but losing fight against a heavyweight champion certainly do not qualify as courageous in the Aristotelian sense. Daring? Yes. Determined? No question.

Awesome? Probably. But there is no moral issue at stake here – nothing of moral consequence to stand up against or for.

In most cases what passes for courage is nothing but mere bravado. In public life we have it in abundance. Noam Chomsky has called George Bush's decision to launch the Gulf war, for example, an act of pure bravado, and recent books on the Gulf war by Rick Atkinson, Mary Moore, Mike Kelly and Milton Viorst seem to support that theory – despite Gen. Norman Schwarzkopf's chronicle (with its accompanying cassettes) of the same event. Nor is such machoism confined to the present time. Medea reduced Jason's braggadocio to absolute silence. After listening to his tales of prowess on the battlefield, she told him that he could not face childbirth once.

Even acts of supreme heroism may not be what Aristotle would have considered courageous. We know, for example, that those who survived life-threatening circumstances in battle to receive a medal of honor for acts above and beyond the call of duty were usually not known for their valor. Indeed, most of them were at a loss to explain what prompted them to do what they did. It was not so much a conscious as an instinctive and spontaneous act.

So much for examples of bravado and spontaneity. What about an example of courage in public life – since it is in public life that genuine courage is most often derided and false courage extolled? The candidacy of Sen. Eugene J. McCarthy in the late '60s strikes me as one of these rare examples.

At a time when no one at the level of presidential aspirancy was willing to challenge the prevailing false gospel of the time (that the war in Vietnam was winnable, that there was light at the end of Gen. Westmoreland's tunnel, etc.), McCarthy went against the grain. He said the war was an example of non-representative governmental leadership at its worst and that it was initiated under the aegis of a false justification (the Tonkin Gulf Resolution), protracted by deception of the electorate and waged in ways that disenfranchised and even corrupted those who were asked to serve. Moreover, he issued this challenge against an incumbent president who was considered invincible at the time.

Later, others would repeat these condemnations. But it was McCarthy who, though he lost the nomination, was the first presidential aspirant to remind the country of its conscience. He did so not once but repeatedly.

How does this compare to the political opportunism evident today? There are many whose primary interest in public life is simply to be an uninspiring part of it or to be the beneficiaries of traditions of public service which they do not exemplify or advance.

In Virginia, for example, we have the example of a senatorial candidate who lied under oath on television – who lied under oath on television before Congress – who lied under oath on television before Congress while wearing the uniform of a Marine Corps officer. Even the president who appointed him continually refers to him as a liar. Ironically, that president's successor and the present Senate minority leader of his party and other of his "Christian friends" take him to their partisan bosoms, assuming apparently that perjury and patriotism are somehow compatible. Here we have pseudo-heroism at its height coupled with sycophancy that plays fast and loose with the good of the country.

Heroism in public life can never be measured simply in terms of victory or defeat. Democracy does not guarantee the triumph of virtue. Phonies can and do win. Heroes frequently lose.

What matters, despite our damnable habit of measuring everything in terms of victory at any or all costs, is the courage of the attempt – the repeated courage of the attempt. If that seems at times to be in short supply, perhaps it is because genuine heroism and courage are always in short supply. But where and when it does exist, it has incredible and undying power. It can change our perception of reality by revealing the truth beneath the appearance. Whatever or whoever can do that can make and change history, and, by extension, the world.

1994

5

ART AND THE STATE

I STAND WITH THOSE who believe that you judge the character of any society by how it nurtures what is best within it. In our United States this certainly must include the arts in all their manifestations since art is the fruit of our highest faculty – the imagination.

Even two-thirds of the preamble to the Constitution enjoins our government (of, by and for the people) to do this: "...provide for the common defense, promote the general welfare, and secure the blessings of liberty to ourselves and our posterity." Fulfilling this injunction certainly does not mean that we stop at the line of national defense. That would be tantamount to a father's teaching his children karate and assuming that this is the extent of his responsibility to them.

But who can deny that the arts can and do promote the general welfare by constantly reminding us of our true selves? And what sweeter gift can liberty bestow if not the climate to create, to perfect through art our imperfect condition and to bring these creations to public attention?

Government support of the arts (assuming that the government is truly us – all of us and not merely the transient elected officials of either party) is actually government supporting itself. Charlton Heston bravely confirmed this in public testimony recently, when he put his reputation on the line by defending the National Endowment for the Arts and urging its preservation. He stated that "art is the bread of the soul."

Regardless of his other political positions, Heston the artist knew instinctively that there are other social hungers beside physical hunger, and he knew as well that art – and only art – feeds those hungers. Of course, some artists and artistic organizations may survive, voluntarily or involuntarily, without government support. But others – by the nature of their needs and purposes – cannot survive without government support when private support is lacking or limited.

In former times this role was filled by the largesse of the independently wealthy (those with money plus taste); they literally formed a state within a state. Imagine what the Florentine Renaissance would have been without Caterina de Medici and her family. It might well have never happened, and all of Europe and the Western world would have been the poorer for it.

Anyone who looks fairly at the NEA since its creation during the Johnson administration knows that its achievements far outdistance its shortcomings. Since any human institution is finite, the NEA may need certain of its procedures reviewed from time to time, as its chairman recently testified, but in the balance the financial or moral lapses occasioned by faulty procedures are minuscule. Speaking financially, let us not forget that the entire budget of the NEA would not purchase the wings and tail assembly of a single F-17 (cost: $300,000,000). Inversely, the cost of one Stealth bomber would fund the endowment for seven years (cost: $1,000,000,000).

As for moral turpitude, suffice it to say that not one charge of legal obscenity has ever been proved in court against one endowment-funded project. And even had there been one or more cases, these would have been traceable to the artist, not the endowment or its impaneled advisors. But these are not the real reasons why some wish to kill the NEA. What they really want is to control not only the means but the ends of the entire process, and in the arts this cannot be done without removing artistic freedom from the equation.

Once a supporting grant is awarded, the ultimate result may be good or bad art, but this cannot be predicted in advance. And in most cases the shadow of obscenity may not be involved at all. Peter Hurd, for instance, was commissioned to paint the official portrait of Lyndon Johnson. Johnson hated what he saw and never permitted the painting to be hung. Similarly the bust of Winston Churchill near Parliament offended Churchill. He thought it made him look like a bulldog. All that can be concluded is that the purpose of art is not to please or condone, but, like modern Parisian architecture, to present an accomplished artistic fact – take it or leave it.

If public taste is offended, all that can and should be said is that any mature society can live with offense without illogically claiming that the government should have nothing to do with funding the arts. I say illogical because the fact remains that the government has been supporting the arts for years: by supporting the Library of Congress (with its poetry readings and other presentations), the National Gallery and, for that matter, public education nationwide, where courses in the arts are part of the curriculum.

Too many people forget that artistic organizations by definition are non-profitable. They survive by solicitation, and they are all destined to lose money as wisely and slowly as they can. Unless they are supported, they pass from the scene. Many are the artistic organizations that hang on by their fingernails from year to year, hoping for an endowment grant to leverage local money into their operating funds.

For almost 30 years I have directed the International Poetry Forum in Pittsburgh. It was funded by a grant from the A.W. Mellon Educational and Charitable Trust, but the bravery of that initial grant was confirmed when the Forum received a small grant from the NEA at the same time. This created an endowing solidarity that permitted our organization to take root, and 29 years later it is still here. To date, men and women from 36 countries (plus our own) have stood on a stage in the Carnegie and recited poems to the eyes of people who paid to hear them. In the process they created poetry's unique and changeless and soul-feeding gift – memorability.

Even if the Poetry Forum were to go out of existence tomorrow, it would leave a legacy of memorabilities that would be difficult to ignore, and that legacy would never have happened if a small endowment grant had not tipped the civic balance in its favor almost three decades ago.

1995

6

WHAT DISTANCE REVEALS

SOME YEARS AGO, when I was in an anti-vacation mood, I wondered why people go away anywhere. Unless they come from unhappy homes, they know in advance that they are going somewhere that predictably is not as good as the place they are leaving. And then there is all the hassle of travel, of packing, of adapting, however briefly, to a different culture, different language, different currency and so on. Why bother?

Despite all my reservations, people voluntarily leave their happy homes and refute my theory simply by going off somewhere. And I, usually reluctantly, include myself from time to time in this number. My only stipulation is that I do not go unless the vacation is out of the country.

Why? I don't exactly know, except that intra-country vacations leave me inwardly unrefreshed – change-of-scene or no change-of-scene. Somehow I must decountrify myself in order to discover my own American culture again and my place in it.

But I remain uneasy about it. Like everyone I am never quite free of anticipating the possibility of an accident abroad.

I know one man who had his leg broken when he was struck by a car in London. I know a woman who slipped in a shower in Moscow and broke her back.

Although both have recovered completely, the accounts they gave of hospital care, hospital costs, ambulance transport and eventual air-travel home were like stories out of Kafka. And, of course, I know that some planes do go down. And then there is always the latent fear, never really dismissible, that something might happen at home.

However, assuming that fate is willing to smile on you and that you are spared the unexpected, you pack your bag one morning and fly eastward through an abbreviated night and arrive, say, in the South of France, in the fabled region of Provence.

Beneath all the glitz and prices, the basic French respect for individual taste as well as the climate, geography and light that drew painter after painter there are omnipresent. Invariably you have pointed out to you the towns or homes where writers, poets, architects and painters lived – Colette, Paul Sinyac, Renoir, Camus, Le Corbusier, Picasso, etc. Many of them are buried there as well. A special pride is reserved for these people, and their graves seem to nail down the landscape. You wonder why this trait is not as deeply ingrained in our country. Why, for example, is the manse of a fallen idol like Elvis Presley treated as a national shrine – while you need the services of an experienced guide to locate the grave of Edgar Allen Poe in Baltimore? Why do we have so many statues of generals and other militarists and so few of those who have imaginatively enhanced our country? Then you turn cynical and wonder if the pigeons would know the difference.

Being abroad is also a time for garnering facts and anecdotes you would otherwise ignore. You learn in one conversation that Shakespeare derived the name of his forest of Arden from the Ardennes. On another occasion you are told about a French tennis player in the '30s who designed a lightweight court-shirt that was subsequently manufactured by his wife's father. Because this player (whose name was Rene Lacoste) liked to travel with luggage made from alligator hide, the alligator (later transformed into a crocodile for some reason) became the shirt's insignia.

You will gather other memorables along the way, and all of these will have a lightening effect on you. But in these lighter moments you will realize that the perspective and marginalia you have acquired have been due in large measure to the fact that you have been spared for a week or so the political and cultural baggage of home. And since you are a tourist in France and not involved at all in the French counterparts of these same problems, you find yourself developing a perspective on your society and your place in it.

Regrettably, distance makes the view clearer and drearier.

How unbecoming for a country as great as the United States to have its time and substance taken up with such unpalatables as urban crime, gun control, security raised to the umpteenth power, the stupidity of drugs, the unchecked degeneration of higher education into the skills of doing and not the skills of being, the persistent pleadings of self-designated minorities of every stripe for rights on demand in lieu of constitutional democratic recognition, the prevalence of fundamentalisms so virulent in matters of religion and politics that one would think there had never been a Renaissance, the killing of the unborn under the guise of freedom of choice, the lamentable way in which racial and homosexual controversies have actually succeeded in almost totally racializing and sexualizing our society so that the generic questions of race or sexuality – instead of personal worth and talent – have become the primary concerns of social life.

All of these illnesses seem to scream out for men and women of courage and vision. But what do we find? Political debate appears to be a scrimmage between the already dead and the not yet born.

And after listening to the current crop of candidates for the highest office in the land, we look long, hard but unsuccessfully for a modicum of bravery, candor, some sense of oratory and, for God's sake, a little redeeming levity and wit.

By the time you reach this point, it's time to return. Your passivity has been cured. Most of the scales have fallen from your eyes.

You bid farewell to a nation whose citizens hold skepticism as an imperative, concluding that this skepticism will save them in the end. My brother got a sample of this a number of years ago when he was in Paris and asked a passing pedestrian if he was indeed French. The answer he received was, "Maybe."

Perhaps this kind of healthy skepticism would be helpful in dealing with our own depressing problems, which seem so similar to those that emerged in the final decade of the last century. The drug of choice then was not cocaine but absinthe.

Women were thought to be engaged in obscene conduct when they abandoned bustles and hoop skirts for what we would call slacks so that they would be free to ride bicycles. The usual nuts were predicting that the end of the world would absolutely coincide with the end of the century.

Regardless, time's odometer clicked inexorably toward 1900. The apocalypse came and went, and the world went on.

1995

7

POETRY'S LICENSE

APRIL HAS BEEN DECLARED National Poetry Month. That April has been so anointed is certainly welcome news, but it remains a mystery to me. By any human standard every month (and every day in every month) should be a time when attention is paid to poetry. Why? Because poetry makes us stop dead in our tracks and appreciate all at once the irreplaceability of everyone and everything.

Irreplaceability. Now there's a word that stands opposed to the usual platitudes we hear about life, particularly in our own country that has made forever legitimate the idea of "built-in obsolescence" (people all too often included).

We hear daily, even hourly, that no one is indispensable. Tell that to the children who have lost one or both of their parents. Tell that to the aging members of that Pirates team of the early '70s when they tried to regroup after the death of Roberto Clemente. The conventional wisdom says that life goes on and, of course, it does. But it goes on thereafter with the scars of undeniable loss. Poetry often memorializes such losses in elegies or memoirs, but its real mission is to affirm and memorialize the present even as it passes, to sing the irreplaceability of this very moment, to be the minstrelsy of here and now. By making us see that we are irreplaceable (and we are, are we not?), poetry says that there is more to life than becoming part of what is called the flow of history. And isn't such a reminder necessary since we live in a society almost totally governed by the clock?

The kingdom of the clock says that people are equatable with their functions, and that is the sum of their worth. The citizens of that kingdom need to be saved from undiluted functionalism by being reminded, as Emerson insisted, that they are who they are before they are what they do – that they are free men and free women before they are doctors, lawyers or Indian chiefs. Whether it is appreciated at leisure (which is what we work to earn so that we can pursue those things that go beyond our functions) or during lunch hours, poetry is such a reminder.

In this sense poems are like letters from our closest friends. They are addressed to us alone. They do not betray or distract. They put us in touch with our true selves. Without poetry we do not have a chance against the pressures of functionalism.

With or without long weekends or annual vacations, the purely functional life resembles the life of the ant. No human being can live the life of an ant since humanity and ant-ness are not equatable. No wonder that most functionaries are turned into tragedians. They look behind and into the illusion called ahead, but they rarely look around. Gradually the route for such a life is predictable – a precise line to a precise spot in a precise cemetery.

No one claims that poetry can help us avoid our mortal destiny. But it can gain us some perspective en route. It can create a momentary vision that clocks cannot kill because poetic vision does not keep that kind of time. A poem is to life what a toast is to a dinner or a celebration. If done well, a toast gives tongue to the mood or spirit of an occasion and makes memorable what would otherwise be forgotten. That's poetry's greatest gift.

A good poem cannot be forgotten even if we try. Try and forget, for example, these two lines from a love poem by John Donne titled "The Paradox": "I cannot say I loved, for who can say/He was killed yesterday?" Try to forget the final line of Louis Simpson's prophetic poem called "To the Western World": "And grave by grave we civilize the ground." How is it possible to forget the concluding image in Randall Jarrell's "The Death of the Ball Turret Gunner?" The brevity of the poem (five lines) seems a perfect match for the estimated life expectancy of a B-17 ball turret gunner in combat (17 seconds): "When I died they washed me out of the turret with a hose." Then there is Linda Pastan's epitaph to a workout on a stationary bicycle: "...this ride feels/much like life itself – going nowhere/strenuously."

Random lines like these stop us cold because they are simply true. We assent to them. By assenting we are turned inward where we are no one but ourselves – not the self that has our name and address and Social Security number, but the self that is in touch with everybody anywhere and always. What other form of human discourse can do that for us but poetry by offering us, gratis, the irreplaceable unforgettably expressed?

The great Cretan writer Nikos Kazantsakis tells a story in which he approaches an almond tree and asks: "Teach me of life." And the almond tree "bloomed." This could easily be a parable for the power of poetry.

Let us assume for the moment that a life which does not "bloom" is a dehumanized life. But if you look into the eyes of someone – a student, perhaps – who has just read a poem that moved him or her deeply and permanently, you see something in the eyes that was not there before. It proclaims a conversion of sorts – a blooming. It's akin to what the postman discovered in the deservedly praised Italian film "Il Postino" when he read the poems of Pablo Neruda. And it's what thousands who saw the film discovered in themselves when they left the theater with Neruda's poems still warm within them.

That sudden blooming comes from the bud of life that poetry's eternal spring nourishes. In April or at any other time, we would be parched and lost without it.

1996

8

CREATIVE STRUGGLE

IN ONE OF HIS FINEST POEMS, Robert Frost addressed himself to the place of work in his (and everybody's) life:

> My object in living is to unite
> My avocation and my vocation
> As my two eyes make one in sight.
> Only where love and need are one,
> And the work is play for mortal stakes,
> Is the deed ever really done
> For Heaven and the future's sakes.

It's not often that one hears work defined as a vocation these days, especially as something that combines the two most basic forces in human existence – love and necessity. On the contrary, one hears work defined as "upward mobility," networking, something to do "for a paycheck," a deal of one sort of another or just a way to occupy yourself while you take your "real life on the side." And most recently work has been made synonymous with entrepreneurism, which means nothing more than having money plus an idea or scheme to generate more money, usually through the work of others.

Of course, behind all these interpretations of the idea of work is the notion that work is what you have to do so that eventually you will not have to do it anymore. In other words, you work so that you won't have to work, and that's the primary and possibly only reason why you work.

None of these concepts of work regards work as an end in itself – a sacred end in itself. After all, the idea of vocation assumes in its very etymology that one is living a life to which one has felt called. That is why people living such a life seem to be a "perfect fit." They look as if their external activity is a perfect reflection of their inner talent and disposition – as if what they do is a reflection of what they are. There is no vacuum between personality and action, no role-playing, no attempt to see work as a means to something else.

Those who regard work as a path to nonworking would prefer to ignore the importance of struggle in human life, and that is a fatal error.

Biologists know that life and struggle are coexistent; where there is life there is struggle – where there is struggle, there is life. Without struggle, life begins to atrophy. If one regards one's work or calling as an ongoing struggle, then the vigor of life is guaranteed. And if one's creativity is part of the struggle, then such a life will have the constant challenge of an adventure from which there is no withdrawal.

All of the aforementioned comments sound a bit moralistic, I admit, but they do affirm that work in the vocational sense has a spiritual dimension to it. In brief, work is more than a job. Whether it be manual labor or craft or intellectual work, there should be something redemptive about it so that one can say, even after one's worst day, that the work was and is worth it. Without that, what does work become but mere toil, a chore, a kind of sentence?

Granted, the idea of work as a redemption has never been widely applauded or pursued in our century. Too idealistic, some say, too far from the reality of day-to-day life. But is it not as deserving of attention as some ideas of work that have far wider currency – work for the sake of the corporation, the state, the collective, the Fuhrer, the Ayatollah, the party, the cause and so forth? Allegiances like these seem to me to be as far removed from the redemption of the individual as can be imagined.

I have no doubt that there are many people in our society who do not have – nor have they ever had – the luxury of choice where it comes to a life's work. They do what they have to do to survive, and so be it.

But those who have a choice must and should, at some point, retreat into themselves and ask themselves honestly what it is that they love to do and what it is that they do best. If the answer to those two questions is one and the same, they should immediately pursue what that choice demands of them. If they do not and choose something of secondary interest, they probably will survive. They may fail, but they cannot excel. If they choose their primary challenge, they probably will survive, they cannot fail, and they can excel. Faced with such alternatives, common sense says that there is only one choice.

Pursuing a vocational choice as one's life work reveals in time that the given world is both imperfect and unfinished. It is ruled by chance and Darwinian forces. It waits for human beings to perfect it, within the limits of the possible. Land, for example, is perfected through agriculture; social relations, through civility and justice; ignorance through education; health through medicine; raw materials through industry and art; culture through the pursuit of excellence. It is as if the God-created world is there for human beings to make something of, hopefully for the better. It is perhaps to this that John F. Kennedy was referring in his presidential inaugural when he concluded his address by stating that "here on earth God's work must truly be our own."

It is widely known that Giacomo Puccini was stricken with cancer while composing his last (and some say his best) opera, TURANDOT. Knowing that he might not live to finish the opera, he asked his students to finish it for him. In fact, he did die while still at work on TURANDOT, and his students did complete what he had started.

When the opera was performed in Milan, Puccini's favorite student, Arturo Toscanini, stopped the performance at exactly the point that Puccini had reached at the time of his death and announced, "Thus far did the maestro compose." He then resumed conducting the opera that Puccini's students had in fact finished for him.

Perhaps that is a fitting parable for what we are meant to be as workers in this world. Continuers. And where possible, finishers.

1996

9

UNSTRAIGHT TALK

RECENTLY, AN EDITOR FRIEND REMARKED to me that the American language was being gutted by the influences of circumlocution, political correctness, legalese and the image-making that is rife in the profitable vineyards of public relations. He added that the results of these weakenings obscure rather than clarify what we try to say. In the end, our public language is debased. The true is made to appear false, the important becomes trivial, the trendy is made to seem permanent, really pernicious effects are rendered benign, and the population is no longer regarded as male or female but neuter.

His observations made sense to me, and I could not help but remember an incident that further proved his points.

A different society ago, I was invited to speak briefly to a group of men and women about to become naturalized American citizens. I arrived at the Federal Building, proceeded to the designated courtroom, took my assigned seat and waited while the citizens-to-be raised their right hands, repeated the oath of citizenship, word by careful word, and sat down as Americans.

They all looked happy, and I noted in my remarks that they were all at that moment as fully citizens of the United States as those whose progenitors had staged the Boston Tea Party.

To further buttress the point I told an anecdote about a naturalized immigrant who was one of a group visiting Ellis Island. Beside him was a woman who at one point gratuitously told him that her forbears had come to America on the Mayflower. The immigrant smiled sympathetically and answered, "That's too bad. I come on a better boat. The Queen Mary."

I thought little of this anecdote until a well-dressed woman approached me after the ceremony and said curtly, "Sir, you slandered my sex in your remarks." I tried to remember if I had inadvertently said something that could have been construed as sexist or even vaguely sexual, but nothing came to me. The woman continued, "In your so-called funny story about the immigrant, you said a woman spoke to him."

"Yes," I answered, "That's what I said."

"You should have said that a person spoke to him," she declared, and left in a huff.

I have often thought of that incident and of its sillier and more absurd descendants (solemn directives to use "vertically challenged" instead of "short"). Simultaneously, I've come to see that this kind of absurdity in our society (or any society for that matter) is the norm more than it is the exception. Political correctness is but its most recent manifestation.

At the level of harmlessness, for example, how does one explain to any child old enough to know his left from his right that people using restrooms do everything there but rest? At the level of hypocrisy, how does one reconcile Newt Gingrich's periodic thumping of the drums of war when he is on record as having himself avoided military service when he was draftable because "I thought I could serve my country better in the future?"

And where is the consistency in renaming the Washington National Airport after Ronald Reagan in light of the fact that this affable, courteous, ceremonious, corny and inaccurate man regarded Washington as the very hub of all our national problems and couldn't wait to return to California?

Everybody knows that euphemism, government misspeak and politically correct diction were invented so that no one would be able to speak vivid American in public. For fear of affronting anyone, all of these perversions of language were justified, not for their elucidation of the truth, but for their power to hypnotize, deceive or schmooze.

The result is that a language as colorless and tasteless as Cream of Wheat has replaced our plain style of public speech. Political correctness and its predecessors have created a vocabulary that really says nothing at all, which may have been the intention of its creators in the first place.

Nevertheless, there remains much that needs to be said, since euphemism does nothing but leave a gaping void where genuine meaning – in either speech or action – is desperately needed for society to function.

What about the real controversies that mere correctness camouflages? For example, is it more important to be politically correct than ethically correct or philosophically correct or medically correct or even grammatically correct? If so, with what justification? If not, shouldn't we instantly initiate real conversations in public life and relegate to perdition the manifestly dull and irrelevant?

Let's face it. Public life is by nature controversial. In light of our individual differences, it cannot help but be. The correct answer is to duke out these differences (intellectually speaking) in the free and open air or on the page as frankly and forcefully as possible. Let the differences speak for themselves.

In such a climate, all that is needed is candor, accuracy, largeness of spirit and, above all, civility. Without an ongoing public airing of our private differences, we are doomed to wallow in recrimination, slander, gossip, wiretaps, small talk and all the rest of the repertoire of the craven and small of soul. The history of our country from 1968 to the present demonstrates only too well what can happen to the body politic when such practices are permitted to debase national life.

Winston Churchill said democracy is the worst of all governments except for all the rest that have been tried. In our addiction to circumlocution and all forms of sweet talk, we have become so accustomed to hypocrisy, leadership by public relations, toady-ism, plain cowardice and blatant wrongdoing in public life that we wouldn't recognize candor and civility if we walked over them barefoot.

If so, the fault (as Cassius said to Brutus) is not "in our stars / But in ourselves." Or rather, our persons.

1998

10

THE INTERNATIONALITY OF GAMES

THE LATE A. BARTLETT GIAMATTI WROTE that one of the ways in which baseball shows it is not governed by clock time is that base runners run the bases counterclockwise. A small point but significant. Baseball innings end only when there are three outs, and if the game goes on until 3 a.m. (as some have), then so be it.

However, though free of the restraints of hours and minutes, baseball, the quintessential American game, is nonetheless subject to the times. And the times change. Indeed, as far as baseball is concerned, they have already changed.

Once a game played at the major-league level only in the northeastern United States and only as far west as Chicago and St. Louis, baseball is now played coast to coast. Moreover, since 1969, the National League has included a team from Montreal. In 1977, the American League based a team in Toronto. There is occasional talk of expanding to include teams from Mexico and the Caribbean. Thus the adjectives – American and

National – are now not only inaccurate, but they may become obsolete.

In addition, the rosters of some major-league teams include players of three races, and the preponderance of players from the Caribbean and South America is no longer limited to exceptional individuals like Roberto Clemente, Mini Monoso, Orlando Cepeda, Luis Aparacio and a few others of their generation.

All of this simply demonstrates that baseball is a democratic proving ground governed by talent alone. If a player is good, he plays, even if he hails, like home-run phenom Sammy Sosa, from grindingly poor beginnings. The result is that players from Puerto Rico, the Dominican Republic, Mexico, Japan and elsewhere are demonstrating their prowess where the "show" is played (and paid for) quite well – in North American ballparks.

This gravitation of foreign-born talent to the country where Abner Doubleday invented the game has met with some resistance only from reactionaries. They feel the game is no longer "native." And, of course, it isn't in the sense in which they understand that term. But these are the same resisters who griped when American citizens from the Negro leagues crossed over into the majors. The nostalgia of these reactionaries for the traditional all-white, American-born major leaguers can simply and charitably be called unrealistic, and that would be putting the kindest face on it.

The crux of the matter is that the centrifugal pull of the United States will continue to draw talent from wherever baseball is played. This is not multiculturalism, as that politically but farcically correct term is understood, but a meritocracy based on a player's talent alone, regardless of his country of origin.

This "return-to-the-source" impulse parallels in many ways what has happened and is still happening to many of the imperialistic nations of the 19th and early 20th century.

The Third World countries that these powers vaccinated with their language and institutions have practiced a colonialism in reverse. Many Jamaicans, Bahamians, Moroccans, Algerians, Tunisians, Indians and others began to look for their futures – in small, or in some cases, large numbers – in the countries that culturally colonized them, i.e. Great Britain, France, Holland, Belgium and the United States.

Take France as an example. The composition of the 1998 French soccer team that defeated Brazil for the World Cup included many former colonials. Two of the winning goals were scored by an Algerian Arab living in Marseille, the very district of National Front leader Jean-Marie Le Pen, whose party opposes immigration across the board and has a purist notion of French citizenship that makes chauvinism look naive. But the team and its victory were embraced by the French people as a whole.

Not surprising in a country that welcomes all who, though not French-born, excel within the tradition and scope of French culture. The French recognize a broader cultural nationality in which, for example, singers like Jacques Brel (Belgian), Charles Aznavour (Armenian), Yves Montand (Italian) and Nana Mouskouri (Greek) have been subsumed into the tradition of French song because their renditions of songs in French are superb. These singers, like many French ex-colonials, are accepted and treasured by French people because their fluency in the language and their artistry and skill meet the exacting standards of French culture considered in the broadest sense.

We Americans have followed a similar pattern regarding foreign-born baseball players who have performed and are now performing in the National and American leagues. What is important to stress is that all of these foreign-born players on American and Canadian baseball teams profess their talent on the field, not by changing the game but by excelling within the existing disciplines and regulations.

Similarly, those ex-colonials who return to or otherwise adopt the cultures of their former imperialistic dominators survive or excel in those cultures, not by transforming them to accommodate their various ethnic inclinations, but by subordinating these to the need of learning the language, arts, practices and customs of the countries and cultures with which they have identified themselves.

The multicultural alternative of presuming that a true culture is the sum of multiple sub-cultures assumes that addition is superior to integration. This actually means that a country of numerous cultures is, in fact, a country with no core culture of its own. Carried to its extreme, the multi-cultural idea leads to fragmentation and, if recent Canadian history can serve as an example, the desire for secession.

Baseball has shown how pastime can integrate players from multiple backgrounds into an identity that transcends their origins. The same holds true in matters of higher culture. Writers like V. S. Naipaul (Indian), Derek Walcott (Trinidadian) and Seamus Heaney (Irish) – all of whom are ex-colonials and two of whom are Nobel awardees – have demonstrated a linguistic mastery that already ranks them high in the annals of 20th-century literature written in English. This is also the case with medicine and science where the primary consideration is the skill and competence of the doctor or scientist, not his address.

It is true in education and scholarship. The aforementioned A. Bartlett Giamatti – Renaissance scholar, Yale University president and commissioner of baseball – is but one example, even though Giamatti made the unnecessary concession to Anglo-Saxonism by using an initial instead of his first name, Angelo.

And it has been demonstrably proved in politics. Look at Fiorello LaGuardia, who is not remembered for the vowels in a name he felt no need to change or abbreviate but simply as one of the best mayors New York ever had.

The answer in these examples, as in baseball, is that deeds speak and will always speak louder than genealogy.

As a man is born, say the genealogists, so he must be. This creates a tribal life without horizons. As a man acts, said Aristotle, so he is. History and the human spirit have proved that Aristotle is right.

1998

11

WHEN VICTORS ARE EVICTORS

"IN A DEMOCRACY, THE HIGHEST OFFICE is the office of citizen." So wrote Supreme Court Justice Felix Frankfurter. If we accept this statement as true (and I for one believe without qualification that it is), how do we as citizens fulfill that office? Obviously and primarily by voting or standing for public office or participating in public discourse by intelligent advocacy or equally intelligent dissent when necessary or simply by daring to be effectively different whenever mindless conformity is in fashion.

We have just experienced an election whose importance had been stressed so often that being reminded had become bothersome. But important it was—no doubt about that. Many who had confused loyalism with loyalty and who conformed to the agenda of George W. Bush were removed from any further handling of the nation's business. In some parts of the country the exercise of the franchise by the electorate was not so much an election as it was an eviction.

Karl Rove and his fellow "geniuses" (how loosely we have come to use that term!) did all they could to de-nationalize and thus localize the election. They tried mightily to compel voters to focus on what was in their and not the nation's interest—an old Nixon trick that Nixon, by perverting Kennedy's memorable line, succinctly packaged when he said, "Ask not what your country can do for you...ask what you can do for yourselves." The voting results showed that appealing to self-interest did not work this time. The Rove acolytes simply underestimated the humanity of the American voter. Who was going to focus on sewer rights or school taxes or the legitimacy of casino gambling against the background of the perverted election results of 2000 and 2004, the rush to war in Iraq that was never justified at the time and remains unjustified to this very moment with the resultant loss of 2837 American lives as well as the wounding and maiming of 20,000 more, 600,000 Iraqi dead and who knows how many wounded and maimed, the expenditure of $11,000,000 an hour to keep the havoc going, the slandering of dissenters as traitors, the proven instances of authorized torture at Abu Ghraib, Guantanamo and clandestinely elsewhere, illicit practices of arrest and detention without charge, cover-ups of the abuses of prisoners in custody, profiling of possible suspects based on ethnicity alone, wire-tapping, home and computer and library searches, and recent grants from the Department of Homeland Security to universities (including Cornell and Pitt) to develop what the NEW YORK TIMES described as "sentiment analysis hardware" to pinpoint negative opinions of the Bush administration in letters-to-the-editor and op. ed. pieces in newspapers and magazines here and abroad. Collectively this record has created what historian Richard Hofstadter accurately called the "paranoid style in American politics" in Washington and throughout the country.

How long could people be expected to swallow the ventriloquisms of Condoleeza Rice, Alberto Gonzales, John Yoo, Charles Krauthammer, William Krystol and the estimable Rush Limbaugh who likened the Abu Ghraib tortures (some of which resulted in sadistic murders) to college hazing and then bravely attacked Michael J. Fox for encouraging stem cell research, for God's sake? How long could the public be expected to ignore the errors of cronies that turned the calamity of Hurricane Katrina into a tragedy of the first order, the indictments of such Bush allies as Kenneth Ley, Tom DeLay, Jack Abramoff, Bob New and Buck Cunningham and the Swaggert-like mea culpas of the evangelist leader Ted Haggard and Congressman Mark Foley? Or did the administration expect people to be oblivious to the fact that during the recent Lebanese conflict the United States balked at a cease-fire while every other nation on earth except England and Israel demanded it or to exonerate Bush's silence when, as reported by Human Rights Watch, between 400,000 and 1,000,000 cluster bombs (all of which were produced by American munitions factories) were illegally dropped on civilian targets in southern Lebanon two days before the war ended?

As if these transgressions were not enough, there was the tacit awareness by millions of people that those who impetuously plunged the country into war in Iraq had never themselves even seen the inside of a military barracks during the

Vietnam War in which they ardently believed. And what of the President himself whose blurred service in the Air National Guard—including an inexplicable leave he was granted to help with the Blount campaign in Alabama—was spent defending Texas from Oklahoma. All of these things could possibly be mitigated were it not for the overcoating of evangelical patina that was used to justify everything from fiscal profligacy to war itself. People became fed up with unctuousness masquerading as piety, religiosity as religion, righteousness and sanctimoniousness as spirituality. In the last days of the recent campaign there were people who could not listen to or even watch the televised cheerleading of the President before the faithful as he excoriated his opponents. This merely confirmed a statement by Henry Steele Commager in 1966: "Men in authority will always think that criticism of their policies is dangerous. They will always equate their policies with patriotism, and find criticism subversive."

The will of the electorate finally caught up with the Bush administration on November 7, 2006. Electronically or otherwise, the voters had their say, and the results speak for themselves. How the new incumbents will change the history of the country is unknown at this time, as well it should be, but the mood of the electorate is now widely known and recorded. It proves that Justice Frankfurter's statement is not only accurate but synonymous with democracy itself where the "highest office is the office of citizen." Always was. Always will be.

2007

12

WHAT WILL HISTORIANS SAY?

DAY BY DAY THE WAR IN IRAQ is being treated as yesterday's news. Pundits, ideologues, retired generals and selective administration spokesmen occasionally have a "take" on the "situation on the ground" (where else could it be but there?), but everyone else is advised to turn the page. Historians, particularly, are rarely asked for their views.

Genuine historians are rarely concerned with "spin." For them the facts are eloquent enough. The following are some of the irrefutable facts that historians have just begun to ponder:

1. The United States invaded a country and deposed a despot. The invasion was unprovoked, the war undeclared, and the end of dethroning a tyrant once supported by our nation was presumed to be sufficient to justify his removal.

2. The defeated country, Iraq, had fallen from 50th in 1990 on the scale of national viability kept by the United Nations to 126th when the war began. International sanctions were the reason for this. The sanctions had a deleterious effect on the

population as a whole, one half of which (or 12,000,000) were children. In military terms Iraq was no match for a superpower.

3. The quick military victory was attributed to total air supremacy as well as the superiority of American technology. The outcome was never in doubt even before the war began.

4. It was demonstrated to the American citizenry and to the world that a pre-emptive war, though branded as illegal, immoral and unconstitutional by a clear plurality of jurists and religious leaders, could be initiated and prosecuted by the President with impunity. Congressional debate (what there was of it) was made irrelevent as were the public protests and dissent of millions in more than 500 cities throughout the world.

5. The case made for war by the President and Secretaries of State and Defense was flawed by fabrication or manipulation of evidence, i.e., tons of uranium supposedly imported by Iraq from Africa (false), uncounted reserves of warheads, chemical weapons, anthrax and botulinum toxin (yet to be discovered), etc. Regardless, these subjunctive claims in the State of the Union Address and before the United Nations had a major influence on the final votes of many members of Congress.

6. The cost of the war is in excess of 20 billion, and the cost of the occupation for an indefinite period could surpass that . The estimate of one general that it would take 200,000 soldiers to occupy Iraq, though viewed as laughable at the time, is no longer considered so.

7. Iraqi fatalities (as was true in the first Gulf War) will never be known. "We don't do body counts of these people," said General Tommy Franks, which implied that Iraqis could

be killed but not counted, which sounds like another way of saying that they did not count.

8. We have created a devastated country with many "untidinesses." Demonstrations and lootings have been called inevitable by the Secretary of Defense, suggesting that such things happen in subsequence, not consequence. Non-competetive bids for reconstruction of Iraqi infrastructure by American corporations have already been secured.

9. The American people have become almost irreconcilably divided with each division savaging the other in the name of patriotism, which is defined by one group as support for the President and by the other as allegiance to the Constitution—echoing similar divisions during the Vietnam era.

10. We have re-enshrined a foreign policy based on global military supremacy. First advocated in the late 1940's by the conservatives of that era, this advocacy persisted until the Russians developed a nuclear bomb when it was replaced by a policy of containment and mutually assured destruction.

11. It is impossible to ignore that the President has underlined the military commitment of his administration for perpetual war by speaking almost exclusively at the service academies, Marine camps, Boeing plants, conventions of major veterans' groups and, at one time, on an aircraft carrier at sea.

12. By an Act of Congress (Patriot I) the government now can, on the basis of suspicion alone, search an American's home without his permission or presence, examine private bank accounts, telephone calls, computers and mail and place him under arrest (without charge) for a time without access to

legal counsel. Patriot II, yet unpassed, advocates not only more of the same but also the indexing of fingerprints and DNA.

Each of these points is a matter of historical record. A conventional and assured military victory may cover a multitude of sins, but historians might have something more consequential to say about these matters which neither flippant denigration nor the passage of time nor any tricks of ideological dry-cleaning can erase. Intolerance of dissent may prevent their conclusions from becoming known for years. In the current climate where intellectual conformity is the rule, contrariness is frequently regarded as betrayal. But if yes-men are doing the accusing, who among us would not want to be among the accused in the name of freedom of thought itself so that the truth can be fully known?

2008

13

REPLACEMENT OR CHANGE?

THOSE WHO BELIEVE THAT VOTING certain politicians out while voting new politicians in is a guarantee of change would be wise to remember the following. In 1968 Richard Nixon won a narrow victory over Hubert Humphrey by inducing the electorate to believe that he would provide an endgame in Vietnam. The war ended in 1973, five years after Nixon's 1968 pledge. Forgotten is the fact that more Americans died in Vietnam after 1968 than before, pledge or no pledge. In the interim the public witnessed the Cambodian bombing and incursion, Watergate, the shooting of students at Kent State, the conviction of Attorney General John Mitchell, the indictment of Vice President Spiro Agnew and others and finally Nixon's abdication in the face of impeachment on the charge of obstructing justice. Voted into office because he promised change, Nixon was ousted from office because criminal charges against him were in the offing , which is enough to caution us that mere replacement now might not mean change but more of the same or worse.

The recent midterm Democratic victories in the House and Senate may turn out to be a redemption, but not if Dick Cheney has anything to say about it. In fact, he's already said it. For him, and assuredly for George W. Bush, foreign policy will continue to be directed as unilaterally as possible by the executive and not the legislative branch of government. In brief, business as usual. What can the newly elected representatives and their colleagues do about it? Since only 40% of the electorate even took the time to vote in what was dubbed a most crucial election (and it was), how much of a change can anyone expect?

How will (or how can) the newly elected Democratic majorities in the House and Senate reverse this farrago with a discredited and callow President still in office, still defending a war agenda that has been declared indefensible by conscientious military men, politicians from both parties and the bulk of the general public, still willing to use "signing statements," wire-taps, torture (insert your own euphemism here), obstinacy and executive privilege to "cut and run" from the spirit and letter of the Constitution of the United States? These majorities will certainly get no help from an appointee like Attorney General Alberto Gonzales who has stated in public testimony that "the (President's) priorities will become my priorities." They'll get no help from the likes of Jerry Falwell, James Dobson, Pat Robertson and other "true believers" nor from mainstream organized religious denominations whose condemnation of the war before it was launched as unjust and unjustifiable was followed by loud silence. They will get no help from neo-cons like Donald Rumsfeld, Paul Wolfowitz, Elliott Abrams, Richard

Perle, Douglas Feith, and the administration's in-house historian of choice Bernard Lewis who, according to George Packer in THE ASSASSIN'S GATE, were convinced as American citizens that the Iraq War "would be very good for Israel," as if the fate and welfare of a foreign country were more important than the fate and welfare of their own. Nor will they be encouraged by those who equate dissent with treason. In this regard David Mamet was absolutely right when he wrote: "We have, as a nation, become our own thought police, but instead of calling the process by which we limit our expression of dissent and wonder 'censorship,' we call it 'concern for commercial viability.'" And, of course, they will get no help from those who insist on political correctness for the wrong reasons. This was the case when Senator-elect James Webb of Virginia, responding to an inquiry from President Bush about Webb's Marine son in Iraq, said, "I'd like to get them out of Iraq." The implication was lost on Bush as well as on those who criticized Webb for rudeness when the man was simply implying that he thought of Marines in Iraq, echoing the title of one of Arthur Miller's early plays, as *all my sons*. What other meaning could there be?

What now dominates discussions about Iraq is unrelenting talk of tactics and strategy, "boots on the ground," re-deployment of assets and such. Conveniently forgotten in the din of proposal and counter-proposal is that this war was and remains an unjust war from its very impetuous and devious inception. And those who launched it are morally and legally responsible for it and should be so regarded by members of the new Congress. It's not a matter of "You broke it, you fix it," in the jargon of Colin Powell, but "You broke it, and now you must suffer the legal and moral consequences by being held accountable for the deaths and suffering caused, the destruction unleashed at home and abroad, the shredding of the social contract in the halls of governance and in the country as a whole, and the shame of exploiting the idealism of thousands of young men and women who have bravely served in a war without end." These are issues that transcend tactical and strategic palaver, and the issues are human beings—there are people standing in those "boots on the ground." It's not so much a matter of win or lose as it is a matter of right and wrong. Regardless of how this regrettable war turns out, there will be no progress until the human dimensions are given their due, which means there will be no progress in our national discourse unless there is moral progress. As Americans we stand for that, or we stand for nothing.

2006

14

THE LAST BRICK IN PLACE: EPITAPH TO A DECADE

SO HERE WE ARE at the end of the first decade of the twenty-first century—penny-pinching Philistines where the arts and education are concerned, procrastinators when it comes to indicting, prosecuting or even raising doubts about malefactors who brag publicly about their malfeasance, more ingoing than outgoing in our social outlook and civic concerns, inured to a daily diet of war and its human tolls, unable or unwilling to challenge the smug morality of the ostentatiously religious and invariably capable of putting in office peevish or undertalented men and women who too often bring the country to its knees. As Horatio said to Hamlet, "We need no ghost come from the grave to tell us this." And we don't, of course. It's common knowledge.

But do all of these failings bracket themselves in a common framework and come from a single source or philosophy? For the sake of argument, if nothing else, consider two Supreme Court rulings as the bracketing parentheses for events from

2000 to 2010. The first was Bush vs. Gore in 2000, and the second was Citizens United vs. Federal Election Commission No. 08-205. Both were 5-4 decisions, and both involved the same or similar Justices in determining the majority decision. The first permitted the 2000 election to go to George W. Bush, and the second permitted corporations and unions to spend unlimited amounts of in support of their candidates. In the latter case money would not go to the candidates themselves but to advertising and lobbying and so on. The effect on the voting public would, of course, be the same.

The Bush-Gore decision did not award the election to Bush directly but in effect stopped the vote count in Florida. Day by day the Bush lead had been dwindling until it could be counted in the hundreds (actually 327), and there were still predominantly Democratic areas (Volusia, Palm Beach, Broward and Miami-Dade) that had yet to be counted, chad by chad. In any case, the Supreme Court vote stopped the Florida count, and Katherine Harris and Jeb Bush quietly proclaimed George W. Bush the President. Affirming that the one-man one-vote principle had been violated, Supreme Court dissenters stated: "Preventing the recount from being completed will inevitably cast a cloud on the legitimacy of the election."

All the above is no secret to Americans nor to those others around the world who closely monitor American elections. Rather than re-hash that, let us consider the consequences. Some say that Bush, Rice and others in government were impervious to the impending possibility of what actually happened on September 11, 2001. For the moment let us leave that to historians. What is now demonstrably true is that the country was led to war for false reasons that were known to be false at the time.

There followed the human costs—4,327 American dead and counting, multiple amputees, suicides and the psychologically and physically wounded. The National Guard has been internationalized while the Marine Corps and the Army have been strained to the breaking point and forced to rely on multiple deployments or to give AWOL service men the choice of serving prison sentences or opting for additional tours in Iraq in order to meet volunteer quotas. Then there is the cost of what is of special interest to the war's initiators and those profiting from it. This has been calculated at $5,000 per second. This translates into $300,000 per minute and onward to $18,000,000 per hour and $412,000,000 per day. The yearly cost is in the neighborhood of $150,000,000,000. Multiply this total by the number of years we have been in theater (seven), and you reach a figure that almost equals the annual deficit, and then you begin to see that the cost contributes mightily to the deficit itself, which in turn shrinks the economy, which, as I have learned from my own experience, in turn impacts the private and corporate foundations that are no longer able to support charities and the arts as they would like. The result in loss for the arts, among other losses in the entire society, is that one arts organization after another disappears.

Of course, our governmental largesse toward the arts cannot be much of a model. The total current annual budget (reluctantly awarded for the most part) for the National Endowment for the Arts is near $155,000,000. This is less than 1% (actually .005%) of the total annual national budget. The cost to the individual tax-payer is thirty-five cents (.35) a year. The federal outlay for what is termed defense (the military services plus their attendant aircraft, ships, tanks, vehicles etc.) amounts to almost one-fourth of the $3,107,000,000,000 national budget. To sharpen your focus, consider that one Stealth bomber costs $1,157,000,000. Repeat: one billion one hundred and fifty-seven million. One plane. This is eight times the cost of the aforementioned annual budget for the NEA. That budget would probably buy one wing and part of the landing gear for one Stealth bomber.

Senator George McGovern, who not only was an elected official in Congress and a Presidential candidate but holds a doctorate in history, has written, as have many others, that we are over-weaponized both conventionally and nuclearly. And years before McGovern made this statement, President Eisenhower presciently warned against the growing power of the military-industrial complex. Since then the complex has only grown stronger. And because weapons and war machinery exist for use in war and grow obsolete when not used, there are many Americans and others throughout the world who are brazen enough to think and ask if the military-industrial complex did not nudge recent administrations toward war as a kind of inevitable excuse to use weapons still in inventory. The Vietnam War, identified as a mistake by its very architects (McGeorge Bundy and Robert McNamara and similarly branded by a younger and more candid John Kerry—"Who wants to be the last man to die for a mistake?") cost the lives of 58,220 Americans alone. For what?

Similarly, in Iraq there was no initial justification, and all those who still believe and say that it was for democracy and not for oil and the security of Israel need a refresher course in *real politique*. Similar invasions to "spread democracy" have a sordid presence in American history from Polk to McKinley to Theodore Roosevelt. And then there is the widely disseminated sentence of former Secretary of State Madeline Albright, "Why do we have a military if we do not use it?" The Chairman of the Joint Chiefs of Staff and the President of Boeing could not have said it better. But waging war for the sake of war has never been a true American ideal, and plunging the country into war for covert commercial reasons is something that leaders do at their peril. And yet it seems habitual that men with third-rate minds continue to send first-rate volunteers to fight and die and be maimed in fifth-rate wars—"serial wars" is David Bromwich's phrase for them. But not one of the champions of our involvement in such wars in the past decade—from the former Vice-President to the former Speaker of the House, Mr. Gingrich—ever volunteered for the Vietnam War although they supported it. Deferment was their war of choice. There's statesmanship for you.

Now comes (or again comes) Afghanistan. Mr. Obama has called it a "war of necessity," but he has not defined "necessity." The outspoken General McChrystal has said he can win the war in a decade, and, if his logic prevails, we can assume that the 30,000 replacements he has been given will be followed by another request, a la General Westmoreland in a previous war, for 30,000 more and so on. The Pentagon, according to historian William R. Polk, is already projecting a war of fifty years in their planning at a cost of trillions. McChrystal's boss, General Petraeus, is on record as calling the war unwinnable, which makes for a curious imbalance of military opinion, to say the least. But the one thing about which there is unanimous agreement is that the central government of Karzai is corrupt. So unless my logic is faulty, this leaves us in an open-ended unwinnable war to maintain a corrupt government at a cost that will further impoverish our already hard-pressed citizenry while at the same time costing the lives of American service men and women and uncountable Afghans. Imagine Marine and Army units going into battle with that mantra as their motivation.

This entire ten-year history of profligacy, cowardice and hypocrisy is a matter of dishonorable public record. What does it say about us as a people? Shall we continue to suffer the consequences of all this lethal folly while ignoring or strangling or short-changing those human energies that give us art, drama, literature, dance, music and poetry? These are the forms of expression that should first and foremost become us as a country and of which they are the deserved and deserving crown. What else but the arts confirms our right to feel what we feel? What else but the arts are capable of showing us who we really are?

Twice in the past decade the voters have attempted to register their disapproval of the war and other policies regarding torture, wire-tapping, illegal detention and a litany of abuses flowing from a policy of "you are with us or against us." The most recent election was a strong rebuttal of what brought us to this point. But the voters discovered that many of the policies which they voted against have been perpetuated. Mr. Obama, who is a lawyer and a former professor of Constitutional Law, promised to go "where the evidence leads." Many contend that knowingly leading a nation to war under false pretences, ravaging a country and destroying a culture could be identified as high crimes and misdemeanors. But to date that there been little effort to mount an investigation. What is the result? If justice delayed is justice denied, then injustice ignored is injustice absolved.

This leads to a consideration of the second bracketing parenthesis to the first decade of the new century—the Supreme Court decision allowing limitless corporate funding for use in political campaigns. Justice Kennedy and his four approving justices said the vote was a victory for free speech. Others saw it as "free speech for sale." Justice John Paul Stevens, speaking for his dissenting four associates, called this a "radical change in the law…that dramatically enhances the role of corporations and unions—and the narrow interests they represent—in determining who will hold public office…While American democracy is imperfect, few outside the majority of this court would have thought its flaws included a dearth of corporate money in politics."

It is as if the final brick has been put in place that began with the election (?) of George W. Bush—an elitist concept of government based on money—not intelligence; on pronouncements—not persuasion; on raw economic and military power used in the service of special interests and global supremacy. What happened after the Court's decision in 2000 made possible the perversion of American promise for the rest of the decade. What will happen henceforth in political campaigning vis-à-vis lobbyists and the rest will be because of the Court's decision in 2010.

In the meanwhile what has become of us as a previously identified open society? From airport screening to mounted video cameras on street corners we have become obsessed with "security." Convincing arguments have been made for the necessity of such oversights (and I for one do not take them for granted), but the effect on our social lives has been to make them more cramped, sour and fouled by the fog of suspicion. Moreover it has made Security Incorporated a big and highly profitable business. As a result, what passes for real love of country is often an affront to patriotism itself—lapel pins, bumper stickers, flags snapping from car antennae, tattoos on biceps or buttocks, souped-up versions of the National Anthem at sporting events and the tag-line of "God bless America" at the conclusion of speeches whose shallowness insults both God and America. And anyone who does not conform to this showiness is seen as unpatriotic and suspect. His Socratic crime? Provoking the reluctant pain of original thought when people would rather succumb to wishful-thinking and blindly hope for the better.

American culture has shown that it is simply better than this. If politics continues to fall short of the true ideals of what America means, then politics as usual (with the benefit of corporate largesse as a legal ally) is not what's needed for a regeneration. Only the arts are capable of doing that. In one of the overlooked but most important of his speeches John F. Kennedy spoke of the importance of poetry and by implication all the arts to America when he said: "When power leads man to arrogance, poetry reminds him of his limitations. When power narrows the area of man's concern, poetry reminds him of the richness and diversity of his existence. When power corrupts, poetry cleanses...The artist, however faithful to his personal vision of reality becomes the last champion of the individual mind and sensibility against an intrusive society and an officious state." We do not hear presidential language like that these days, but an "intrusive society" and an "officious state" still need to be confronted by what the arts—and *only* the arts—can offer us so that we can see them for what they are. And act accordingly.

2015

15

PARADIGM LOST

Many assume that chronology and history are the same. Chronology is basically a listing of happenings in the order of occurrence. The order is sequential, not consequential. Once the events are dated and recorded, they are relegated to the definite past like last year's desk calendar.

Historians, however, look for patterns or relationships between events. If something happens because something else made it happen, then the relationship is consequential. Linking cause and effect is the historian's way of understanding how the past perpetuates itself in the present. Where the chronicler stops is where the historian begins.

As we enter the second decade of this century (TIME magazine called 1999 to 2009 "The Decade from Hell"), three major alterations have been initiated that directly effect the judicial, legislative and executive branches of government and could have lethal consequences for democracy itself.

At the risk of repeating the already overdone, consider the election of 2000. Forget the usual counterarguments, i.e.

Gore won the popular vote nationally, Enron flew in lawyers on corporate jets to obfuscate the outcome, office help came from Washington to create mayhem during the recount, etc. The crucial point to remember is that the law of one-man one-vote was suspended when the Supreme Court stopped the recount before it was finished. Because there was no final count, the Court literally awarded George W. Bush the presidency on a 5-4 vote, a ratio that continues to this day. Whatever the justification, this created a precedent whereby for the first time in our history a presidential election was determined not by voters but by Supreme Court Justices. Actually by one Supreme Court Justice. Justice Stevens said ominously in his dissent: "Although we may never know with complete certainty the identity of the winner in this year's Presidential election, the identity of the loser is perfectly clear. It is the Nation's confidence in the judge as an impartial guardian of the rule of law." He meant, of course, that a precedent had been set, and that the consequences were unforeseeable. Bush's press secretary at the time, Ari Fleischer, spoke to the chronicler, not the historian, in each of us when he brushed aside the dissenters and their supporters with, "Get over it."

The second most disturbing Supreme Court decision (also by a 5-4 vote) was the ruling that fiscal support of candidates by corporations deserved the same First Amendment protection as free speech. Here we had a ruling that equated an organization whose primary purpose is to realize profit for its officials and stockholders with every citizen's right to express himself or herself on matters of public policy. This in effect elevated corporate funding to Patrick Henry status. As a result, corporate contributions in the billions to corporately favored candidates swayed many contests in 2010. The implication that was drawn by many was that the corporately supported winners would be expected to return the favor. An estimated 67% of senators, for example, are millionaires who could not be expected to vote for higher taxes on the rich, etc. The result, as some assert, is an oligarchic government dominated by a rich ruling class.

The third disturbing factor was the reluctance of the judicial and legislative branches of government to curb the actions of an omnipotent presidency. Relying on "signing statements" and its own pliant Attorney General, the former administration flaunted its lapel-pin patriotism by initiating and prosecuting two wars now universally seen as illegal, by legalizing torture and multiple forms of unlawful surveillance on private citizens, by approving imprisonment without charge and other unsavory practices. Many of these have been inexplicably continued by the Obama administration, despite campaign promises made to the contrary. The results are that the lives of Americans and nameless others are lost on a daily basis in a pair of wars that have been dubbed "endless," that the open society we should be has been shrunken by an obsession with security and that we have become in part a debtor nation, many of whose foreign policies, particularly in the Middle East, seem more indebted to illusion and injustice than to American self-interest.

Some say that these three distortions of the polity are the prices to be paid for peace. Some on the right say they are destined to further impoverish us so that we will be "regrettably forced" to cut programs like Social Security and Medicare to pay our way out. Some say that they are deliberate attempts to shrink the middle class so that we will create an up-to-date version of feudalism. Some say, some say…

If the past can be said to have created the climate where these aberrations were possible, then those chroniclers who turn their back on history are the modern amnesiacs. The Obama decision, for example, to "look ahead" and not hold accountable those responsible for our current state was not magnanimous but unjust and foolish. It perpetuated the very vices it promised to end. And the same might well be said of anyone who thinks that the follies of history can be "dry-cleaned" away. They can't be, and they won't be.

2015

16

THE COMBAT BEGINS WITH NO

IN 1944 ALBERT CAMUS WROTE a series of columns in the clandestine resistance journal COMBAT in which he described how many Frenchmen truly loved "their country in silence while silently despising its leaders." Although this was understandable, he warned that people would end by saying "...this does not concern me...I live in the country, and the end of the war will find me just as I was at the beginning of the tragedy...living in peace." For Camus this represented a defeat, and he further warned that it could lead to degeneration unless his countrymen strove toward a time when contemplation converted itself to action.

History does not treat exact parallels kindly, but the atmosphere in our country today is not far different from what Camus was describing in 1944. Despite all the spin and the miasma of fear that the Bush administration is so good at spawning, it has been and is becoming more readily apparent by the day that we are being governed by manipulators. Whether it is the President's inner or outer circle or neither is irrelevant.

The result is that this manipulation has bred a distrust of government itself, and the accumulated effect has not only made radical changes in our social life but in our very mentalities. We go to airports as if we are heading for a dental or medical examination. We are more than casually concerned about surveillance of all kinds as our private lives are more and more invaded or threatened with invasion. We act like people who are waiting for trouble to happen, and the President regularly spurs these fears by releasing "previously undisclosed intelligence." Regrettably, we do not pit real intelligence against such "intelligence," and, as Camus correctly anticipated, we drift toward the fringes of the present tense in the hope that our problems will pass as all things pass.

I suggest that such inclinations are degenerative to our national character and that they have been initiated or encouraged by people who deserve neither our confidence nor respect. Can anyone view a discredited subaltern like Alberto Gonzalez and have any confidence that justice is being served at the Department of Justice? Can anyone regard the initiatives of Richard Perle, Paul Wolfowitz, Scooter Libby or Douglas Feith (described by General Tommy Franks as the "dumbest (mother's son) I ever met") as anything but homicidal to the people of Iraq? In light of the verdict of historians, generals, the Baker Commission and the bulk of the electorate, who can explain why the President and Vice-President go on indulging in swagger, motivational speechifying and partisan cheerleading without a hint of grief or regret? (Even the pro-American recently elected President of France has called the war in Iraq a regrettable "historic mistake.") And what of Condoleeza Rice's dream of "a new Middle East" after she and the President did not halt the Israeli onslaught on Lebanon until more than 1,000 were killed while roads, runways, bridges, water plants, Beirut neighborhoods and whole villages were destroyed? And what of her and the President's denials of the use of torture on detainees long after the Rumsfeld memorandum authorizing such torture was made public? Surely she and the President knew that men are capable of anything when they have other men or women at their mercy and that every President from George Washington on had condemned torture as barbaric and un-American for this reason?

All of these are lethal follies, and men and women in their prime are paying for them daily with their lives and limbs. If such governmental misguidance is not enough to engender everything from disgust to outright rage, what else is needed? In the face of such mendacity and the tragedy it has created, is it possible just to look the other way and somehow hope for the best? When we saw mediocrity rewarded with the nation's highest honors, as with George Tenet and L. Paul Bremer, we looked the other way. Even when we understood that the principal beneficiaries of this war were the oil interests, the military industrial complex, the ongoing repressive policies of the Israeli government (which we have dutifully replicated down to plastic handcuffs, blindfolds and hoods in Iraq) and the so-called "religious" base of the Republican party, we looked the other way. Even when we witnessed flagrant photo-ops of the President at the various service academies or when we learned that the military dead were returned covertly to our country when they should have been publicly extolled along with their next of kin by the President himself as heroes for being asked to do the impossible, we looked the other way.

At this writing a majority of the acquiescent Democratic and Republican members of Congress have signed on to let the war continue in its present status for the summer (while the Iraqi Congress is on vacation). What else can be expected except more of the same, which means more losses of American and Iraqi lives. Surely, this a time when contemplation should be transformed into action! But if so, how? If the usual avenues and methods of participatory government have been rendered ineffective to reflect the will and consent of the governed, is it enough to love one's country in silence while silently despising its leaders? At the moment this seems small consolation, if that. But one thing can be done. In one of his major works Camus stated that we do not know who we are until we know what we can say "no" to. Such a "no" must be said at the time when it is required and not subsequently, and it must be as irrevocable as it is deeply personal and definite. From that point on the "yes" of our lives can be said to begin; we know then who we are. Theodore White once wrote that "one man plus the truth equals a majority." A majority of one is usually ignored, but a majority of one raised to the millionth power cannot be. And if the "yes" of each of those lives converts itself into significant action whose exact nature may be unknowable right now, all the power in the world will not be able to silence or thwart it. But first the "no" must be said. And meant.

2007

17

COMING TO TERMS WITH TERMS

NATIONALITY AND RELIGION are two of the most controversial words in American political life. The controversy arises from misunderstanding, and the misunderstanding is caused by how each is defined—or ill-defined.

The nation to which you owe your allegiance defines your nationality. If you are a bona fide citizen of the United States, your nationality is American. If you are a citizen of Canada, you are a Canadian. If you are from Finland, you are a Finn. As a United States citizen you are immediately identifiable as such when you travel abroad. Your passport attests to it. When you fill out visa forms, you write *American* in the space reserved for nationality. Ironically this does not carry over into civic life in the United States. Some years ago I conducted an exercise with a group of thirty college students when I asked them one by one to identify themselves by nationality. And one by one the wrong answers came: Polish, Irish, German Irish, Italian, Greek and so on. Of the thirty, only one student identified himself as an American, and he was a transfer student from Harlem. The other twenty-nine told me candidly that I threw them off by asking them to tell me their nationalities. They assumed that nationality and ethnicity were the same. I then referred them to the true meaning of nationality, which in our country has nothing to do with ethnic heritage. It is based solely on allegiance to the Constitution as amended. When first proclaimed in the eighteenth century, this was a revolutionary concept. While the people of other countries had a genetic, racial or ethnic blood-base in common, the United States based citizenship on assent to the constitutional principles of its founding. It has rightly been called an experiment in governance. And there are some who say that such an experiment could well fail because a common ethnicity is absent.

I have already indicated that many Americans have no hesitancy in identifying themselves as such when they are abroad, but who define themselves by their ethnic heritage when they are back in the States. It seems ironic that an American should feel more American in Europe than in Pennsylvania, for example, but such is often the case. I do not make this point as a matter of chauvinism, which I find an obnoxious vanity, but as a matter of observable fact. In political life the fudging of citizenship and ethnicity is now part of the DNA of national elections. Voters are identified by hyphenation in blocs: Italo-Americans, Afro-Americans, Irish-Americans, Hispanic-Americans and so on. Politicians who target audiences in this way do not do the American experiment a favor. In fact they contribute to the dumbing down of the electorate by appealing not to the mind but to the blood. And any student of history knows the mischief that can come from that. Even more mischievous is the existence of dual citizenship, which boils down to the fact that a person can be a citizen of two countries simultaneously. No matter what practical advantages this designation may have for some, it strikes me as being as contradictory and ill advised as bigamy.

The relationship of religion and citizenship is even more combustible. With regard to political life the founding fathers were deists, i.e., they believed in God conceived as the primal source of creation, the "Supreme Dispenser of all Good" and other such absolutes. Though Christians by and large (with the exception of Jefferson who swore "hostility against any form of tyranny over the mind of man"), the founders were adamant in their belief in the separation of church and state. Regardless, they were unequivocal in their support of the First Amendment to the Constitution which affirmed that "Congress shall make no law respecting establishment of religion or prohibiting the free exercise thereof, or abridging the freedom of speech , or of the press." This clearly meant that they were *for* religion per se. (Washington himself believed and so said that any citizen's contribution to the common good sprang from religious and moral impulses.) But they wisely separated the religious spirit in man from what we would call institutional religion or ecclesiastical authority. It was with regard to institutional religion (*any* institutional religion) that they believed in the separation of church and state. And based on historical precedents they had good reason to think so. For this reason it was common and commendable for elected officials then and thereafter to invoke God's blessings on the American experiment but in terms that did not ascribe the invocation to any particular church or sect. Washington: "…that Heaven may continue to give you the choicest tokens of its beneficence." Lincoln: "… that this nation, under God, shall have a new birth of freedom." Kennedy: "…"God's work must truly be our own."

The guarantee of diversities of religious belief (as opposed to those countries with only one state religion) resulted in a multiplicity of religions throughout the country, which is exactly what the founders intended. It was for this reason that President John Adams signed and the Senate ratified in 1797 a treaty that stated that the "United States of America was not in any sense founded on the Christian religion." The obvious inference was that the country stood for freedom for citizens to choose any religion or none and remain in absolute adherence to the First Amendment.

As disconcerting as this seems to be to fundamentalists of all stripes, it happens to be the law of the land. And, allowing for the usual hypocrites and fanatics who violate the spirit of the law and who are eventually perceived for what they truly are, the law has worked. The wall between secular government and religious institutions has remained while simultaneously creating the climate for the religiously motivated to work and debate and of necessity compromise in a democracy that makes such actions possible.

It may seem redundant to review the true meaning of nationality and religion in our public life, and it may very well be, but clarity, even at the cost of belaboring the obvious, is something that there's never enough of. Especially if confusion and arrogance and messianism, as we have experienced in the first decade of this century, are the only other alternatives.

2009

18

THE WAY OF THE BOOK

AT SOME POINT IN THE TWENTIETH CENTURY a generational divide happened. It created what I choose to call the generation of the book and the generation of the screen. The generation of the book included those whose first encounters in life were with the page. The generations of the screen were those whose first encounters were with the screen (television or motion picture) or the monitor. The book generation probably retained throughout their lives the impression that the page had a certain primacy, that a number of pages when gathered and bound into a single volume represented something complete, that these volumes, even in the days when acid-free paper was the exception in publishing, had a definite permanence. The generation of the screen usually considered the page just another medium on which words could be printed.

Since I am of the generation of the book, I have asked myself if the page is indeed just another medium. If it is, then books in all probability are destined to share the fate of cuneiform, clay tablets or papyrus—previous media that had their moment in the sun and were eventually eclipsed. But if not, why not?

What is it about books themselves that give them an almost sacrosanct permanence, whether it be the BOOK OF KELLS, incunabula or the text, trade or children's books of our own and other decades? For lack of a better word I claim that the staying power of books is that they all possess bookness. Although it is never wise to include the word to be defined in its definition, I can find no substitute. The bookness of any book invites us to enter it, consult it, make its contents our own and remember it in a way that is both unique and intimate. Compare the different expressions on the faces of those who are reading with those who are facing a screen—any screen. The reader's expression seems by its very nature more private while the expression of the other is less so, however slightly. As long as books are capable of creating this intimate sense of privacy—a one-to-one sharing of the thoughts of the author with a reader whose total attention makes the sharing possible—, then books will endure because there is really no substitute for them. The screen does not seem capable of doing this. In a speech delivered several years ago at the University of the South, the present Librarian of Congress James H. Billington explained why as follows: "Television and its even more isolating offspring, the computer, are subtle promoters of loneliness. They discourage communication between people even as they foster the illusion that everything an individual needs is easily at hand through the click of a mouse."

I do not mean to denigrate the many advantages of the screen in any of its forms. Motion pictures, television, the monitor and the modum have goodly assets that books do not and cannot possess. But often the more the screen gains in notice, the more it loses what I have identified as intimacy or privacy. Its range and informational capacities are extraordinary. Its reach is international. Its accessibility is instantaneous. But if genuine books are, as one poet has called them, "letters from our closest friends," then books possess by their very nature what screened truth cannot give us.

Despite the fact that book sales are now alleged to be bountiful, it is statistically a matter of record that fifty percent of the literate population of the United States does not read a single book over the period of a year. (The literate and the total population are not synonymous. Ten years ago, for example, approximately thirty percent of the population of Philadelphia was said to be functionally illiterate.) Of the remaining fifty percent, approximately thirty-eight percent read a single book. This leaves some twelve percent that read more than one book a year. What can we conclude but that the majority of people in our country get their knowledge from the screen—television predominantly—or from spin-offs like the pictorial magazine? Anyone who has followed the demise of newspaper after newspaper in American cities in the last fifty years cannot help but see the decline of print journalism in favor of screened news. And in screened news the language is largely interlocutory—transitioning what is shown on the screen or simply backgrounding it. One researcher estimated that the spoken words in a thirty-minute national news program averaged out to a a single printed column in a newspaper like THE NEW YORK TIMES.

The great asset of the screen is that it creates recognition. The great asset of the page is that is begets understanding. If understanding and the wisdom it is able to engender are the true goals of human knowledge, then the reading of books is the indispensable and perhaps only way for such wisdom to happen. Everyone with an incipient interest in etymology knows, for example, that the Latin word *libera* is the root of such English words as liberty, liberate or liberal (as in liberal education). But the root of *libera* is the Latin word for book—*liber.* Apparently the Romans believed that there was a connection between books and liberty. They were quick to recognize that books put minds in motion, and that a mind in motion was capable of pursuing the truth wherever it led, and that such a pursuit could free the pursuer to make up his own mind. What else is freedom but that? What else is liberal education but the formalization of this pursuit, and what is it built on but books—"greats" as the Oxonians called them or, as identified by such educators at Robert Hutchins, Mortimer Adler, Stringfellow Barr and others, the great books? The goal is intellectual freedom. Free men and free women are those who read books, learn from them, discuss what they know in a spirit of open disquisition and arrive at their own conclusions and judgments.

I heard a retired librarian proclaim on one occasion that all books were people once. I would amend that to say that all books are still people. Each book is a legacy or an autobiography waiting to be shared. This inspired one surgeon to write that no one should consider himself educated unless he reads at least fifty books a year outside of his field. Translated, this makes the reading of books synonymous with intellectual nutrition itself. It does not mean reading with what one writer described as the "immoral speed of the professional critic." It means reading thoughtfully and, above all, steadily. The mind needs to be fed, and books are its nourishment.

As an addendum it should be mentioned that books as objects offer us more than opportunities to read. Even in the era of quickprinting, bookmaking remains a craft. Books are the unified results of the efforts of authors, designers and printers. A book that is well designed and printed invites our attention and our admiration as much as a good painting or a superb sculpture does. It exists as the handiwork of man. I am not a bibliophile as that term is usually understood, but, speaking personally, there is something in the very heft of a book held in hand that creates a pleasure that nothing else matches. For me a library of such books suggests a special kind of genuine wealth, and its value does not diminish with time.

Because books are made by hand ("manufactured" in its etymological core meaning), their composition, design and production evoke in us something resembling love. As owners or borrowers, we have all faced rows of vertical, horizontal or askew books on a shelf and heard every book whisper quietly to us, "Read me." Whether we own books outright or take them out on loan from libraries, which are places where the dead have left their first and last living wills and testaments, we develop a bond with them every time we read or re-read them. The deeper our love is for a particular book for whatever reason, the deeper the bond. All of us have finished reading books which we could not put down or want to see end. Such books became part of us. We could no more imagine throwing them away than we could see ourselves scrapping a keepsake from someone we truly love.

Putting bookmaking, book ownership or book borrowing aside for a moment, what should our response be to Robert Louis Stevenson's remark that a truly educated person is one who could be stalled for hours in a train station without a book and not be bored for a minute. Bypassing the pleasure that a person might derive from just looking around in such circumstances, I would say that evading boredom would be directly proportionate to resources that book-education had previously endowed him or her with and which are able to be tapped at will. If memory is the library of the mind, that library is always open for consultation at any time. In the already mentioned speech by James H. Billington, these prescient lines make the same point, but better: "Books are and will remain our principal guardians of memory: of the anguish and aspirations as well as the achievements of those who have gone before. Mute witnesses from the past are often better guides in life than talking heads in the present. In our dialogues with other living people there are always games going on—politics, psychodrama, showmanship, who can talk the fastest. But, alone with a book, one finds imagination is the only limit. Boundaries are not set by someone else's pictures on a television screen; thoughts are not drowned out by someone else's sounds on a boom box."

At those times in our intimate association with books when imagination is "the only limit," it is common to encounter moments when we discover phrases or sentences that we cannot forget even if we try. We often find ourselves coming back to them or even quoting them time after time. They bequeath to us what John Bayley identified as "the inevitable solace that right language brings." I have many books in my own personal collection that qualify, some of which have passages or even pages which I have marked, underlined or embellished with marginalia because I wanted to keep them permanently in mind. Here are just a few examples that I thought important when I first read them and still regard as important now.

Rudolph Arnheim: "Animals that survive by escaping danger have their eyes on the sides of their heads, whereas those who live by attack have frontal eyes. This suggests that man, with his frontal eyes, is a creature of initiative rather than response—initiative being the human version of attack."

Jacques Barzun: "Great populations without a god outside themselves will turn to national war or race hatred to find the glow of common sacrifice and the call to transcendence that the human spirit requires."

Hunter S. Thompson: "In a closed society where everybody's guilty, the only crime is getting caught. In a world of thieves, the only final sin is stupidity."

Thomas Hardy: "Literature is the written expression of revolt against accepted things."

Yakub Ibn Ishak Al-Kindi: "We should not be ashamed to acknowledge truth and assimilate it from whatever source it comes to us, even if it is brought to us by former generations and foreign peoples. For him who seeks the truth, there is nothing of higher value than truth itself; it never cheapens or abases him who searches for it, but enobles and honors him."

Jerzy Kosinski: "It took Napoleon to figure out that with the cubic content of just one Great Pyramid one could fence France with a barrier one foot wide and ten feet high—an achievement not even his Napoleonic brain could conceive of."

William Shakespeare (from KING JOHN): "Grief fills the room up of my absent child, lies in his bed, walks up and down with me, puts on his pretty looks, repeats his words, remembers me of all his gracious parts, stuffs out his vacant garments with his form....Thus have I reason to be fond of Grief."

Albert Camus: "There is always a philosophy for lack of courage." "Those who write obscurely have great luck: they will have commentators. The others will have only readers, and this, it seems, is worthy of scorn." "Mental chastity—prevent your desires from straying, your thoughts from wandering."

John Ciardi: "You judge a man by what engages his attention." "Games are human activities made difficult for the joy of it."

These passages have remained with me not simply because they express genuine truths about life itself but because their memorability is made possible by exactness of expression. Not one of them contains what T. E. Lawrence once identified accurately as "passenger words."

Who was it said that we do not know what we know until we try to write it? Writing—real writing—is not the same as saying. However spontaneous it may appear, writing comes into existence after a period of distillation. It is capable of being revised until we reach that moment of exasperation or satisfaction when we think we've come as close as possible to what we mean. Ernest Hemingway once said that "hard writing makes for easy reading while easy writing makes for hard reading." The "hard writing" to which Hemingway was referring has the stuff of durability about it, and it is books that preserve it. In this age of email and faxes, both of which are indispensable when instantaneous communication is necessary, the mode of communication called "snail mail" is regarded as a step backward. Yet I wonder how many authors of our time will be remembered for their collected faxes or emails. On the other hand I know for sure that the letters of Flannery O'Connor, Janet Flanner or Archibald MacLeish will endure for as long as human beings appreciate what writers write when they put pen to paper to express what they think they know or feel. There is something about the veracity of a handwritten letter that is absolutely authentic, and when such letters are gathered into books they can be suddenly transformed into literature. People who read them often feel that the letters were written to them (or are at least understandable by them) even though they were not the original recipients.

I fully accept the fact that the libraries of this day and age are facing the challenge of preserving books that seem destined for eventual decay. Not the subject matter of the books, mind you, but the materials themselves—paper, bindings, ink and so on. There is a certain sadness in this. I have had to rely on microfilm for occasional research when the primary source was no longer available, and I suppose this might become more and more the practice in years to come. But a library of microfilm is somehow not the same to me as a library of books. Again Mr. Billington: "A library in a home or a public place takes us out of our noisy, hurry-up, present-minded world into Keats's world of 'silence and slow time.' Libraries keep alive the values of the book, which favor active minds over spectator passivity, putting things together rather than taking them apart, privileging dreamkeepers over imagemakers. Whatever the confusion of our mind and the profusion of our information, things can still come together in a book—just as the left and right halves of the brain come together in one human mind, and the hemispheres—east and west, north and south—in a single fragile planet."

One of the pithiest comments I have ever read about the importance of books was made by Irving Cobb when someone surveyed his voluminous library and asked him provocatively if he had really read every book. Avoiding the provocation but not the opportunity for a riposte, Cobb responded, "Some of them, twice."

2007

19

IN DISPRAISE OF FOLLY

He told me that he had just completed his third tour overseas—one in Afghanistan and two in Iraq. He was in his early twenties, an Air Force mechanic, and he was on leave to introduce his fiancée to his family in Ohio. We were seated side by side on a flight from Memphis to Pittsburgh.

When I asked him his opinion of the war in both Afghanistan and Iraq, he paused and said he just listened to both sides of the argument. I did not pursue the point since I felt instinctively that he was saying what I was probably expecting him to say. I had had conversations like this before with some of his contemporaries, and they invariably ended in silence. In the military where compliance and obedience are inculcated. what could a young enlistee on active duty say if he were really opposed to the war, and to what purpose? General and staff officers conspicuously kept their reservations to themselves until they were safely retired. Sounding off while in uniform invited either reprimand, penalties, courts-martial or all three.

Still I could not help but admire this young airman's composure as well as the sense of trust he had in the system as compared with those officials in the administration who were using the system to suit their own ends. The latter simply would leave it to the military to implement what the administration wanted, and subsequently let the military pay the price for it.

Putting aside my political reservations with the current administration's policies in Afghanistan and Iraq and in the Middle East as a whole, I tried to force myself to focus on these neo-patriots and their acolytes simply as people: Cheney, Perle, Feith, Wolfowitz, Ledeen, Addington, Kristol, Gaffney, Fleishcher, Snow, Libby and the rest. Most if not all of them had never experienced first hand a day of military discipline or understood the toll, both physical and spiritual, suffered by men and women in combat and after combat. Their constituents were their fellow deferees, cronies, corporate insiders, lobbyists like Abramoff and his kind, AIPAC, Fox News and the righteously tunnel-minded from the tribes of Jerry Falwell and Pat Robertson. These were the kind of people in public life who seemed to think that they were beyond disquisition, rebuttal or even the irrefutable laws of logic, and their sangfroid was often capable of driving those opposed to them to naked rage, even fury. At times some Americans could not stand to look at or listen to them on television, and this revulsion included and frequently began with President Bush, whose reputed reliance on his "gut" decisions created the impression that the man believed the seat of reason was not in the brain but in the lower bowel.

I asked myself how such a cadre of well-paid, well-positioned and well-connected idealogues could have gotten such a strangle-hold on American foreign policy, particularly in the volatile Middle East when their allegiances to Big Oil and the Sharon agenda were and still are widely known. They could hardly have been considered impartial. (As a matter of fact, what have their initiatives created in Iraq, Gaza and Lebanon but actual or incipient civil wars, which has led some to conclude that this might well have been the very purpose of these initiatives. Has anyone ever considered that wayward possibility as true?) Why had they never been confronted to their very faces (and this did not exclude the President) with a challenge similar to how one enlisted man questioned Donald Rumsfeld in Iraq? The soldier asked frankly why he and his comrades had been sent into battle without sufficient armor for their Bradleys. Rumsfeld's flippant answer was that "You go to war with what you've got," as if the war's start had not been impetuously chosen but forced upon us. Why had the President and the Vice-President linked the invasion and occupation of Iraq to Al Qaida long after no such link was known to exist? Indeed, even the laws of logic denied the very possibility of a connection since Saddam Hussein was a secularist while Osama bin Laden was a revolutionary religious zealot. Both men had nothing in common but a mutual hatred. Putting aside for a moment the Downing Street Memo that proved conclusively that the pre-invasion "intelligence" had been made to fit the decision to invade, why did no one express doubt when the President blamed his decision exclusively on "bad" intelligence? And if the intelligence provided was flawed, as the administration stated, why had George Tenet, the very head of Central Intelligence, been given the highest civilian award our country can give for providing it? The same could be said of L. Paul Bremer who, after disbanding the Iraqi army and doling out non-competitive contracts to Halliburton and others to create four mega bases in the country, actually gave the insurgency its genesis and turned the American presence in Iraq into what Thomas Ricks identified as a fiasco. Bremer, like Tenet, was similarly rewarded with the nation's highest civilian honor for what is now considered a complete misreading of the situation, And all during this time the office of Attorney General John Ashcroft was hyping the country with heightened alert after heightened alert that created a miasma of social fear that made logical discourse as rare as the courage of citizens to initiate it.

As tiring as it is to review all of these blunders and cover-ups for the millionth time, the time it takes to do so is not time wasted. Putting aside for the sake of argument all of the snafus that have brought us to our present condition, why had simple logic never had a say in repudiating the reasons for the war in Iraq in the first place? Forget the zero result of inspections for the moment and the sane, irrefutable warnings of Scott Ritter and others. Was it logical for the President to place approximately 150,000 troops in Kuwait as a perfect target for Saddam Hussein if he actually suspected that Hussein had a nuclear weapon? Surely he knew that the Hiroshima bomb in 1945 had killed 200,000 people in twenty-five minutes and thousands more in the days and weeks thereafter through radioactivity. Knowing this, only a fool would jeopardize American troops less than fifty-five nuclear years later by placing them next door to Iraq unless he knew all along that no such weapons existed the first place.

And then there is Dr. Condoleeza Rice who, along with the President, repeatedly denied that torture was used during interrogations in Iraq, Afghanistan and Guantanamo. She and the President persisted in such denials even though a written order from Secretary Rumsfeld authorizing the use of torture during interrogations became public. In effect Rumsfeld's order confirmed the ongoing use of what was being denied by the White House and the Secretary of State, thus denying the denials. The public was left wondering if the logical laws of contradiction had been temporarily suspended in the District of Columbia.

In regard to torture as an officially mandated policy there can little doubt that torture is totally at odds with American jurisprudence and accepted military practice. Despite claims by Alan Dershowitz and others, there is no doubt that torture, regardless of the reasons given for its being used, dehumanizes the torturer. Someone has written that there is nothing that one man cannot do to another, particularly if one man has another at his mercy. Journalists like Mark Danner and Naomi Klein have described in detail what prisoners have been subjected to by American interrogators or guards and what other prisoners have endured during what is euphemistically called "rendition." The photographs from Abu Ghraib left nothing to the imagination. Here were naked men hooded, chained, threatened by dogs, beaten and otherwise subjected to the entire chromatic scale of pain. And the pain was not only physical. Sleep deprivation, illumination around the clock by strobe lights, confinement in closet-like cells, being masked with women's underwear and flooded with high decibel metallic music for hours on end were standard operating procedures. Some prisoners lost their minds under these regimens. According to Naomi Klein, the multi-year solitary confinement of Jose Padilla in a seven by nine foot cell with all the attendant psychological punishments of heightened sound and either bright illumination or total darkness has made it doubtful if he is fit to stand trial. And finally television's DEMOCRACY NOW showed guarded prisoners in a group being forced to masturbate. Adding to the humiliation was that they were forced to do so in front of female guards. How it is logically assumed that such practices advance the national interest is a subject well worth pursuing, however offensive it might be to public sensibilities.

All of these matters were on my mind as our jet from Memphis came in for a landing in Pittsburgh. The young Air Force mechanic and I parted company with a handshake after he told me that he was scheduled for a fourth tour in Iraq. For many days afterward I could not stop thinking about him in his situation. I knew that he and thousands like him had volunteered either out of ardent and genuine patriotism or with an eye for a collegiate education or to receive special training or for the lack of any other promising alternative. They had every right to believe that their willingness to serve would not be exploited. But regardless of motivation, by volunteering they placed themselves under orders, and orders are only as wise as the person or persons who issue them. And what have these orders created but death, misery, braggadocio and folly?

Since 2000 we have seen our country under the governance of men and women who seem to lack a tragic or a historical sense where the most serious international problems are concerned. Their officially adopted policy of "anticipatory self defense" has no ethical or logical basis at all and recalls Lloyd Bensen's paraphrase of a previous administration's foreign policy as "ready, fire, aim." But where are those in public life who can somehow reverse what has been so tragically set in motion? Are there any prospective leaders who can compare with FDR, George Catlett Marshall, Dwight Eisenhower, James Forrestal or J. William Fulbright? As for allies, who are experienced and selfless enough to see and say where we are headed? Was Tony Blair on his best day ever comparable to Winston Churchill or Harold Macmillan?

It is no small feat for a citizenry to find its way to the truth in an era of lethal folly and fear hyped to the highest power. Thousands of uniformed Americans have already been killed or maimed in the name of both. And a possible future victim could be a young Air Force mechanic who was looking forward to introducing his fiancée to his family while simultaneously facing a fourth tour in a war zone. But Americans, like any other people, cannot live in the permanent state of fear that this administration has done so much to instill and prolong. The truth of the matter is that such fear can only remain dominant if people refuse to awaken and hate what they fear more than they fear it. That is happening now, however belatedly. But such eras are not new in our history. "It is part of the general pattern of misguided policy that our country is now geared to an arms economy which was bred in an artificially induced psychosis of war hysteria and nurtured upon an incessant propaganda of fear." This is not a statement blogged on MOVE or excerpted from the agenda of Veterans Against the War. It was made by none other than General Douglas MacArthur in 1951. As a warning it was as timely then as it is now. How we respond to such a warning will have much to do with what kind of a people we are or will become.

2011-2015

20

THREE OF A KIND

Hillary Rodham Clinton, Madeline Albright and Condoleezza Rice were the secretaries of state in three administrations. What seems undeniable now is that they had a similar inclination toward or reaction to the use of military power either by the United States or by an allied, client country. They also were alike in that they claimed that military force should be used only when all other options were exhausted. That, of course, is a standard refrain used by all those who are already determined and committed to the use of force, regardless.

Hillary Clinton, as is now known to the point of boredom, voted with the George W. Bush administration to invade Iraq. The result of that invasion was that more than 400,000 Iraqis were killed and more than that wounded (mostly civilians), approximately 5,000 Americans killed and more than 32,000 wounded both physically and mentally, 2,000,000 Iraqis displaced, Iraqi culture irreparably damaged and fragmented (libraries, museums, antiquities and relics were destroyed and the population divided along religious or ethnic lines), the Iraqi army summarily disbanded (thus providing the backbone for ISIS) and a lackey government installed that was a government in name only. Mrs. Clinton has recently (and opportunistically) called her original approval a "mistake," but that does not exonerate her from the consequences of her original decision. Her vote meant that she thought *replacing a foreign government, good or bad, was our right simply because we had the power and the pretext to do it.* You cannot "dry-clean" that and act as if what you approved in principle was subsequently a "mistake."

Also as Secretary of State, she encouraged vigorously the "leading from behind" campaign to destroy the Qaddafi dictatorship in Libya. This again was regime change seen as an American right. Libya remains in shambles today with rival factions battling for control and with ISIS moving into the void. When told that the dictator Qaddafi had been captured and reportedly bayonetted through the anus and shot, Mrs. Clinton replied dispassionately, "We came, we saw, he died." Then, as actually recorded on YouTube, she laughed.

As evidenced by her recent speech at the annual AIPAC convention, Mrs. Clinton's close ties to Israel and Israeli policies show little hope for evenhandedness in a Clinton presidency. With her Super Pac already in receipt of more than $5,000,000 from Israel-firster Haim Saban and her pledge before her AIPAC audience that Prime Minister Netanyahu would be the first person she would invite to the Oval Office in the event to her election, the electorate can expect little to be changed. American vetoes at the UN will go on blocking reprimands of Israel misbehavior, the annual billions will continue to flow to Israel, the illegal settlements will continue to expand to make the possibility of a dream-like two-state solution more and more unlikely, and the Palestinians will continue to suffer simply because they are who they are. A recent caricature of Mrs. Clinton as Israel's lawyer is not far from the truth, but that is no more laudatory in an American President than her "So be it" pledge (never denied) that she would not condemn the next Gaza onslaught even if 200,000 Gazans were killed.

Madeline Albright showed similar disregard for Middle East realities in a televised interview in 1996 with Lesley Stahl regarding the cut-off of medical and other humanitarian aid to Iraq via a UN resolution initiated by the United States. Lesley Stahl reminded Ms. Albright that the consequences of the cut-off resulted in the deaths of more than 500,000 children and that this number actually exceeded the number of children killed in the bombing of Hiroshima. "Was it worth it?" Ms. Stahl asked. Ms. Albright pondered the question and then said, "We think it was worth it." Her answer raised quite a few eyebrows subsequently, but nothing came of. it. She was even awarded the Medal of Freedom in 2012.

Finally, there is the example of Condoleezza Rice. Like Hillary Clinton and Madeline Albright, she has an impressive dossier: Baccalaureate and Doctoral degrees from the University of Denver, a Master's degree from Notre Dame, piano skills of concert quality, distinctions in academia, politics and business, her name on an oil tanker, Secretary of State and assorted subsidiary roles in the George W. Bush administration, post-administrative honors, degrees, citations, speeches priced as high as two hundred and seventy thousand per speech. (Not quite in Hillary Clinton's category but more than pocket change.)

Her defense of the Iraq War and of torture never quite disappeared nor did her insistent prolongation of the Israeli War that was sanctioned by her and her Decider-in-Chief and the servile and obsequious Lord Tony Blair. A border skirmish was cited as the provoking cause of the war, but subsequent evidence revealed that the war had been planned for months as a way of crushing forces in the south of Lebanon that were seen as a threat to Israel. The Israeli attack was not confined to the border or even to the south of Lebanon but included the country as a whole for collective punishment. (It was the same strategy and rationale that was used against Gaza in 2008 and 2013).

Results? More than 1,000 civilians killed, one million displaced, bridges and roads destroyed throughout the country, airport runways cratered, water refineries hit and a coastal oil refinery bombed. The oil-slick from the refinery's tanks and pipes fouled beaches in Lebanon, Syria, Turkey, Greece and Cyprus for years. Two million cluster bombs (made in the United States but with the stipulation that they could not be used against civilians) were dropped on southern Lebanon, and many still remain a decade after the war. More than thirty-nine people, mostly children, have been killed by them to date.

Dr. Rice convened with Israeli authorities when the war ended after 28 days, although every country in the world with the exception of the United States, England and Israel voted in the United Nations that the war should have stopped three days after it began. She proudly proclaimed the birth of a new Middle East and prepared to fly to Beirut. While she was en route, the President of Lebanon, surveying the destruction and ignoring protocol, told her not to land.

Former Secretaries of State Clinton, Albright and Rice seem to have shared a disturbing preference for the use of force, whether by the United States or by allied or client countries. Some have said that all three are visceral hawks. Whether they are so in fact or were simply following the orders of their superiors is for historians to determine. But all three should have been told that talking or acting "tough" and then using force and military power to prove it when you are on the wrong side of an issue is indefensible. And as the defenders of that policy that has made the Middle East what it is today, they bear the responsibility and the guilt.

2014

21

A FAREWELL TO ARMS

AL CAPONE was not just whistling Dixie when he identified guns as equalizers. If a dwarf's enemy is a giant, and the dwarf is armed, the odds favoring the giant vanish. That's equalization. Inadvertently or not, single-minded pro-gun activists have since made a creed of this word coined by a convicted, syphilitic murderer and crime-boss. To them it is sacrosanct.

Some have traced the love affair that many American males have with guns to our frontier beginnings. Necessity then begot two traditions: the armed and determined lawman (Wyatt Earp and his "High Noon" successors) and the armed outlaw (Billy the Kid and eventually the aforementioned Capone.) Both of these traditions still exist in enhanced versions perpetuated by Hollywood and the creators of the Marlboro Man and others fantasies. But a third tradition now exists with them—the armed citizen. Making light of the Second Amendment's insistence that citizens may possess firearms when involved with militias, gun-owners now may do so as individuals because the Supreme Court has confirmed their right as settled law.

Anyone who has had any experience with firearms understands how lethal they are. Police officers, detectives, soldiers, sailors and Marines (based on my own experience) are trained intensively in the use of weapons and treat them with care and respect. They know what they can do. But firearms that are bought legally by citizens may end up in the hands of those not trained in their use. Petty squabbles and frustrations, ranging from gang shootouts and turf wars in ghettoes to the Columbine and Virginia Tech massacres, are often settled by gunfire, and murderers grow younger year by year. Add these incidents to others involving illegally procured weapons, and you have a major social problem. It is estimated that there are approximately 300,000,000 firearms in the United States, exclusive of those illegally owned, and this is a conservative figure. There are some 80 homicides and suicides by gunshot in the United States every day. This comes to slightly less than 30,000 per year. Senator Frank Lautenberg of New Jersey has extrapolated the figure of 9,000 homicides in America each year from this number and compared it with 200 such crimes or less per year in most other countries (excluding Mexico, Turkey and South Africa). Also, in a related study where countries were graded for their record on gun control, the United States received a grade of D across the board. Japan, one of many in the survey that received an A, makes it illegal for citizens to own a "firearm or sword." This makes weapon ownership there not a right but a *crime*. (Homicides by gun in Japan last year were 35.) To insure compliance Japanese police are authorized to search any home where the presence of weapons is so much as suspected. Leaving statistics, law and NRA sloganeering aside for the moment, what is it about guns that makes them particularly attractive to some men? The poet William Matthews has gone so far as to call guns "the jewelry of men." He may have a point. A less poetic inducement would be that guns give a gun-owner a sense of power (the equalizer factor). Then there is the belief that weapons relieve gun-owners of fear. But can they really do that? How can a gun protect someone from a drive-by shooting (even if the target is as protected as the White House), a surprise break-in, a sudden marauding rampage similar to one that wounded Congresswoman Gabrielle Giffords and killed six others, a planned mugging or an assassination?

One of the regrettable attitudes created in a society where civilians can be armed is that one's fellow citizens are no longer seen as neighbors but possible adversaries with whom you may have to deal lethally at some point. I leave aside the concomitant vigilante mentality that goes with this together with the belief that the righteous gun-owner is willing to fight the government itself if his Second Amendments rights (as he sees them) are not respected. All this leads back to what constitutes manhood for American males. Is it the hyper-virility way of the warrior in our ongoing war-culture or the rites of professional athletes thumping their chests in triumph after a tackle or a score and pointing the forefinger of a heavily tattooed arm at some Valhalla in the sky or the customary Hollywood avenger-types plus Superman, Batman, Spiderman and other cartoons or the late Charlton Heston vowing to keep his uplifted rifle until it is pried from his "cold, dead hands"? The emphasis here is on resolving controversy through force—physical force initially and lethal force ultimately. But is this genuine manhood or simply *machismo*, which the Spanish define and regard as bravado masquerading as courage? In any case, it is doubtful if not impossible to build a social contract of mutual trust between citizens on that.

Without any further consideration of the basis for a gun-culture, what conclusions can be safely drawn from the annual harvest of gun-deaths as we have them? It seems to me that the facts make their own arguments. If an essentially gunless society like Japan (and there are others) has an average of 30 gun-deaths a year while the United States has 80 per day, it seems logical to conclude that widespread gun-ownership just might have something to do with it. A key sentence from the Cullen Report on Arms Control would seem to confirm this: "Homicide rates tend to be related to arms ownership. Everything else being equal, a reduction in the percentage of householders owning firearms should occasion a drop in the homicide rates." Is this logically correct? Yes. Will it change how most people think about this subject? Probably not. Regardless, the legally protected rights of gun-owners as well as the inflated and misguided definitions of what makes men men will persist as the underpinnings of the culture that sustains the kind of armed society we have created for ourselves.

A much more worthy description of a genuine citizen was given in 1899 by a largely unknown chronicler, poet and musician named John Walker Wayland. He wrote that a true man was one "who does not make the poor man conscious of his poverty, an obscure man of his obscurity, or any man of his inferiority or deformity; who is himself humbled if necessity compels him to humble another; who does not flatter wealth, cringe before power, or boast of his own possessions or achievements; who speaks with frankness but always with sincerity and sympathy; whose deed follows his word." This strikes me as a description of a man in full, but those who believe in gun-justice will surely regard the ideals expressed here as overly optimistic, even naïve. There are no allusions to any arms or other power assets to supplement what philosophers call the "courage to be." It's a coda of life for the brave. Such bravery does not guarantee triumph or even survival. Just dignity.

2011

22

A MYTH IS AS GOOD AS A MILE

A MYTH BY DEFINITION is a story or notion that is partly true and partly false. The falsity permits the truth to be stretched, and the truth makes the falsity acceptable. Take the myth of knowledge, for example. It is assumed by many that someone who knows a lot is by that fact alone intelligent, whether that knowledge has been converted into wisdom or not. But how many of us know "knowledgeable" people who have exercised terrible judgment, proving that there are many well informed but stupid people in this world. And what of the myth of war? Some see it as the testing ground of the mettle of the young, ignoring that war is essentially what Albert Camus said it was and is—legalized murder, strangers killing strangers. Seen as anything but that, war, even if judged necessary or inevitable, is distorted into something other than the tragedy it is. And what of the myths surrounding wealth, longevity and manliness, which are three of the major myths of our time?

It was Ronald Reagan who said at the dawn of his presidency that he wanted "a country where everyone could be rich." Horatio Alger said it better, but the meaning is the same, and the basic meaning is that being rich means having or wanting more money than you need. In short, wealth. Apart from the fact that this is mathematically impossible for "everyone" in our own or any society, it caters to the desire of many always to have more. It feeds on the envy of the "have-nots" for the "haves," and it taps into what is commonly and mistakenly referred to as the myth of the American dream.

No one denies that having enough money to meet one's needs is not only desirable but essential. However, unless accompanied by something once called munificence, over-abundant money often becomes a problem, a burden, an indulgence or, in the case of the insatiable, a vice whose real name is greed. The so-called "trickle down" theory was a rationalization of the hope that the wealthy would see to it that their wealth flowed back or "down" into the society from which it came. The problem was that it didn't "trickle" down but often "trickled back up to the "tricklers" or their cronies. Exceptions to this practice were few.

For those in our country who believe that we live in an economy and not a society, the possession of money is often seen as a measure of life itself. How frequently have we heard, "How much is he or she worth?" If the person has a million, he is assumed to be worth a million. If someone has nothing, he is assumed to be worth nothing. In other words, the bad side of the myth of wealth affirms that a man who has no money has no being whatsoever.

Longevity or "long-life" has as many mythical dimensions as can be imagined. They all originate from our natural desire to live on or, as one actress put it, "to die young when you're as old as possible." Consequently, when anyone dies, the usual comment of the survivors is that he or she died "too soon." This is based on the assumption that living to threescore and ten and possibly beyond is almost regarded as a right. Of course, life's logic rarely obliges our expectations. It is a matter of existential fact that we die either from disease or violence. Some would argue that we also can die of age, but the cause usually can be traced not to age alone but to an age-related disease or malady. This leaves the end of life determined by disease or violence only. There are no alternatives, and neither disease nor violence has a birthday. But mythology does not easily accede to actuality. People still seek the Fountain of Youth a la Ponce de Leon, insist that their bodies be frozen in death in the hope of an eventual re-incarnation or contribute mightily to the fortunes of the vitamin, cosmetic or plastic surgery alternatives. Myth becomes more attractive than fact, nine times out of ten, even though it is fact that eventually and inevitably prevails.

The mythology surrounding manliness, particularly in our society, is fraught with confusion,. It is often identified with a profession—the military, various sports, police work, ranching and so on. The idealized American hero looks something like the eternal Marlboro man, astute in his saddle, ready for anything and capable. His cousins in caricature are Superman,

Tom Mix, James Bond, Rambo and various loners created for the screen by John Wayne and the early Clint Eastwood. All are rooted in the myth that masculine strength is decisive and supposedly indomitable. It explains much of the attraction of body-building and the kind of cock-of-the-walk strut that George W. Bush and other aspirers feign in public. It's what's on display when a basketball player or football player scores and points one forefinger at the stars. But true manhood eschews display. Even in the military where bravery in the face of adversity is expected, the ultimate accolade is for altruism. The Congressional Medal of Honor is reserved for those who gave or risked their lives for others—bravery for the sake of life, not supremacy. And the same kind of concern for others, which is the ultimate manly virtue in any way of life, is evident in other less ultimate but no less considerate ways. I remember a Hollywood ceremony when Gregory Peck was given a lifetime award for his work in film. Numerous directors and actors appeared to offer their praise or thanks. When it came time for Peck to speak in acknowledgement, he thanked each in order and then, turning to his wife in the audience, said, "You're the only one for me, Veronique. I'll see you later." And finally, there is the example of the former President of the University of Notre Dame, Father Edward Malloy (known to one and all as "Monk" Malloy). Learning that his nephew needed a kidney to survive, he immediately volunteered one of his own, saying rather offhandedly, "I only need one anyway." If real manliness does not exist in these few examples, I would be hard pressed to find a more apt word to describe it.

Whether the subject is wealth, longevity or manliness, it goes without saying that myth plays a major role in how we define all three. To separate truth from falsity—fact from myth—is an ongoing challenge, and it never ends.

2009

23

POWER AND PRETENSE

IT IS IRONIC BUT TRUE that power in its most obvious forms is the least enduring while power in its least obvious forms is the most enduring. For proof consider the following. If asked to define the essence of power, most Americans (and indeed most people throughout the world) would equate power with strength. They would say unhesitatingly that they would consider any nation (the United States, Russia or China, for example) powerful if it possessed formidable military assets. By the same standard they would consider any nation weak whose military strengths were in comparison negligible, i.e., Lebanon, Denmark or Switzerland. At present the United States of America is considered the most powerful nation on earth for the simple reason that its military assets are second to none.

But if the capacity to endure is the hallmark of true power (and I for one believe that it is and must be), then history demonstrates again and again that so-called "powerful nations" frequently had a short lifespan before their power waned or was superceded by a "stronger power." In 1926 Paul Valery wrote: "In modern times no single power or empire in Europe has been able to stand supreme, to dominate others far and near or even to retain its conquests for longer than fifty years. The greatest men have failed to achieve this object, and even the most fortunate led their countries to ruin: Charles V, Louis XIV, Napoleon, Metternich, Bismarck: average span— fifty years. There are no exceptions." Valery easily could have added the names of Hitler, Mussolini and Tojo, and his conclusion would still apply since Hitler's Reich, Mussolini's fascist Italy and Tojo's militarized Japan lasted for mere decades. And the USSR could also be added to the list since bolshivism from the time of the Russian Revolution to the time of its implosion in the nineteen eighties spanned just a fraction more than a half a century. Today there are some who say that our own country's military adventurism in Vietnam, Afghanistan and Iraq may be following the same historical pattern. The obvious conclusion that can be drawn from these examples is that military supremacy as an enduring manifestation of power does not guarantee longevity. Indeed, when military supremacy is used only to instill fear in those who have been conquered or occupied, the seeds of resistance have already been planted. At a certain point the conquered will hate what they fear more than they fear it and rebel.

Even those who continue to believe in military superiority as an emblem of national greatness are forced to admit that such supremacy in our era is finally synonymous with technological superiority—not valor or the customarily esteemed virtues of the warrior. But even technological superiority extracts a price in human terms. In a prophetic book entitled OF

FLIGHT AND LIFE that he wrote in his later years, Charles Lindbergh described an incident when he was piloting a Lockheed Lightning P38 back from a raid on Palau in the South Pacific. Flying in formation with three other P38s, he was suddenly attacked by a Zero. The Japanese pilot had completely surprised Lindbergh and would have shot him down had not the other three pilots joined the battle and saved him. The incident taught Lindbergh that he had survived because the Lightning was a better plane than the Zero, which could not out-maneuver the American pilots. But he concluded years afterward that a victory guaranteed by science was not sufficient since "in worshipping science man gains power but loses the quality of life." And he added presciently: "Was science's power of survival only temporary, capable of winning battles but not of saving man?"

Of course, history demonstrates also that power conceived only as force (technological or otherwise) has often been bested by prowess, luck or guile, which proves that military power has other opponents beside counterpower. Prowess: the slow and weighty warships of the Spanish Armada were regarded in their era as invincible. But they proved no match for the lighter and more maneuverable vessels commanded by Sir Francis Drake, who became their nemesis. Luck: in the battle of Tarawa in World War II, the Japanese commander was killed purely by chance before the invasion by an incoming round while he was moving from one command post to another. From then on the Japanese forces were leaderless at the top. The fierce battle lasted for three days, but the outcome was never in doubt because the Japanese forces were left without a central command.

Guile: according to Homer and Virgil, the Trojan War had been fought over ten years to a standstill when Odysseus convinced the Greeks to conceal soldiers inside a huge wooden horse, which would be offered as a gift to the Trojans. If the Trojans accepted the ruse and brought the horse within the walls of Troy, the concealed soldiers could emerge and open the gates of the city to the main Greek force. The trick worked, and Troy fell. Call it guile, if you wish, but the victory was a victory of intelligence over strength. For a contemporary parallel in guile consider the heavyweight title match between Muhammad Ali and George Foreman in Zaire. For eight rounds Ali permitted himself to be pummeled at will by Foreman in what came to be called the "rope-a-dope" strategy. The more powerful of the two, Foreman punched and punched until he was spent. At that point Ali struck, and the fight was over. Again, a victory of intelligence over strength.

Speaking of intelligence, how can the enriching of natural intelligence in the quest for knowledge not be regarded as one of the most powerful factors in what is called human progress? From the time of the invention of the wheel to the advanced surgical knowledge that permitted a surgeon recently to remove cataracts from both my eyes, insert crystal lenses and reward me with 20-20 vision with no need for glasses, the power of knowledge is an enduring history of possibilities that became facts. And their staying power—their ability to endure–has become as beneficial as it is indisputable—not only in scientific terms (medicine, architecture, aeronautics, agriculture and so on) but in the human disciplines and the arts as well. What gives literature its staying power but its affirmation of the permanent truths of human nature and its capacity to touch the human spirit everywhere and at any time? Why are plays like MEDEA and ANTIGONE still in repertory after two thousand years but solid proof that a woman wronged by her husband is capable of deeds far beyond our imagining or that a sister who has to choose between love of her brother and compliance with an arbitrary state regulation will choose love even if her choice results in her own death? Why are the ILIAD and the ODYSSEY still read except that they show how life always means a departure from home, a struggle with whatever forces await us (in war, in education, in business, in politics, in everything) and then hopefully a return to the home we left? Why does the tragedy of ROMEO AND JULIET still resonate (and will always resonate) but for the fact that we sympathize and identify ourselves with lovers who come together by choice and not to accommodate a family's or a community's wishes? And who among us cannot identify with what the anonymous Anglo-Saxon author of THE SEAFARER wrote about the risks of sailing: "But there isn't a man on earth so proud,/So born to greatness, so bold in his youth,/Grown so brave, or so graced by God,/That he feels no fear as the sails unfurl,/Wondering what fate has willed or will do." Perhaps it was for this reason that Ezra Pound, from whose translation of THE SEAFARER from old English I have excerpted these few lines, could and did say that all poetry is contemporary, which frankly means that the ongoing presence of poetry in particular and literature in general has no past tense. That is where the power of literature lies—in the presence that words create when they are read or heard. And that presence is invariably undeniable and enduring. One need not be a sailor to sense what the author of THE SEAFARER is implying in the lines I've quoted from his poem, namely, that fate never absolves us of our fear of the possible no matter how pride, destiny, youth, bravery or blessedness has favored us. That fear is universal, and we recognize and feel it in the poet's words. This is what Robert Frost confirmed when he wrote: "The right reader of a good poem can tell the moment it strikes him that he has taken an immortal wound, that he will never get over it. That is to say, permanence in poetry as in love is perceived instantly. It has not to wait the test of time. The proof of a poem is not that we have never forgotten it, but that we knew at sight that we never could forget it."

This naturally leads to a consideration of the power of education since it is as a result of education that we were exposed to those subjects upon which our culture rests—poetry, of course, included. We were first educated by our upbringers, who taught us everything from basic hygiene to good manners. Then came professional teachers from whom we learned the basics—the American language, history, mathematics, the natural and social sciences, the disciplines of various sports and so on. After high school, when we would no longer be pupils but voluntary learners or students, there would be more history, more literature, more science and the rest of the canon. I am speaking here of liberal education where truth is pursued for its own sake and where our natural appetite to know is an end in itself. This is where minds are born, and the power of teachers to put such minds in motion is in fact the gift of gifts. Once in motion the mind seeks truth on its own momentum, pursues it to its multiple sources, rids itself of superstition and seeks the ultimate prize— intellectual freedom. The seeker is then truly liberated and lives the life of a free man.

History is rife with legacies of teachers whose names survive not in bronze entablature but in the lives of those who were the beneficiaries of those who generously shared their knowledge: Socrates, Tertullian, Minicius Felix, Erasmus, Bernard of Clairvaux, John Henry Newman, Robert Maynard Hutchins, Mark Van Doren, William Sloan Coffin and Sarah Johnston. Sarah Johnston, you say? Never heard of her. How does she deserve to be listed among the luminaries? This is how. Tom Lincoln, the father of Abraham and Sarah Lincoln, lost his wife, Nancy Hanks, to a cattle-born transmittable "milk disease" when Abraham Lincoln was nine years old and his sister but slightly older. Being a dawn-to-dusk farmer, Tom Lincoln desperately needed someone to rear his two children. He was told of a widow named Sarah Johnston who lived in Kentucky with three children of her own. In due course Tom Lincoln went to Kentucky, proposed to Sarah Johnston and brought her and her two daughters and son back to his farm in Indiana. There she developed a special love for Abraham Lincoln, taught him to read and write and gave him his first books, i.e., PILGLRIM'S PROGRESS, AESOP'S FABLES and the King James version of the BIBLE. Had Nancy Hanks lived, she certainly would not have been capable of giving Lincoln what Sarah Johnston gave him since she as well as her husband were illiterate. In retrospect, we can rightly wonder what would have happened to Abraham Lincoln without Sarah Johnston? He probably would have remained a farmer like his father. He certainly could not have been a lawyer, a congressman or the President of the United States had it not been for the love and tutelage he received from Sarah Johnston. And had Lincoln not been President at the time of the Civil War, the United States of America might not be the country as we know it today, And all of this was because of the love and care that one woman had for a son who was not even her own. And yet, despite the debt that all Americans owe to Sarah Johnston, there are too few who know who she was. My guess is that Sarah Johnston would really make light of this. Like all who act out of selflessness and love, she undoubtedly regarded her affection for Lincoln as an end itself, proving that love is its own reward. But the powerful consequences of that love outlived both Sarah Johnston and Lincoln himself and have repercussions to this day in the lives of all Americans and anyone else conversant with American history.

In a recent feature article in NEWSWEEK Jon Meacham stated that the word for power in Latin is *imperium*. This enforced the basic theme of his article in which he concluded that power or *imperium* was "at heart the capacity to bend reality to your will." The inevitable conclusion that one is forced to draw from Meacham's thesis is that power is ultimately coercive. Whether achieved by force, money, deception, seduction or training, the aim is to compel people to do what you want them to do. If this sounds more than vaguely fascistic, the reason is that it is. My belief is that genuine power is derivative in the fullest sense not from *imperium* but from the Latin verb *potere* and its French descendent *poeir*. The meaning of power here can best be translated as "to be able" or "to enable." The imperial meaning of power as coercion is not even implied. In this sense the enabling of Lincoln by Sarah Johnston fully qualifies as the true meaning of power. Hers was a selfless act of sharing what she knew with young Lincoln and making it possible for him to continue to learn as he grew, relying on the basic skills and appetite for learning that she had instilled and awakened in him. It is the same impulse that motivates parents and teachers at all levels of education, and its power can never be underestimated.

I would argue that this same transformative power is one of the many beneficial capabilities of the arts, particularly the arts of music and poetry. Both music and poetry seem to have the power of putting those who are exposed to them in touch with their deeper selves. How this happens is truly a mystery, but we know that it does happen when the imagination of someone is inspired to manifest itself in song or words so that the listeners or readers are changed by the experience. Consider the esteem in which the French chanteuse Edith Piaf was held by the French people before, during and after World War II. Physical beauty had nothing to do with her appeal. Here was a woman who not called a sparrow for nothing; she was diminutive, eschewed opulent wardrobes on stage and seemed indifferent to cosmetics. But she had an unignoreable and quintessentially Parisian voice that was the voice of France for more than half a century, and she holds a permanent place in the French pantheon of song that can only be described as timeless. Her death had such a crushing effect on the internationally famous author Jean Cocteau that he said he no longer wished to live. Such was the effect (or power) that one woman's voice had on one man.

And Cocteau and others listened to Edith Piaf as others do to this day because of something in her songs that touched and still touches them. And the same can be said of the legendary Egyptian singer Om Khalsoum. She was revered not only in Egypt but also in Lebanon, Syria, Jordan, Iraq, Saudi Arabia, Yemen, the Emirates and across North Africa. Her appeal was to women as well as men, but particularly to men who seemed almost mesmerized by her songs. She had created the custom of presenting a concert once a month in an open theater on the banks of the Nile. By mid-afternoon on the day of the concert many businesses, stores and government offices would close so that the owners or employees could ready themselves spiritually for the evening. It was said—not quite in jest—that if she were invited by an Arab head of state to perform in his country and refused the invitation, that government would collapse on the following day. When she died, it was a time of national mourning among all the Arabic-speaking people and beyond. And as a final tribute, it was estimated that more than 4,000,000 (4,000,000!) people came to her funeral in Cairo.

Like music, poetry has the same irresistible power to awaken the self that exists deeply within each one of us. Like music, its true power is the power to endure unforgettably. It would not be farfetched to claim that words spoken or written so as to qualify as poems are actually immortal. They not only never die, but they stay alive in their original form. Many whose lives are "immortalized" by having buildings, colleges, airports, ships, towns or even whole cities named after them cannot rival the immortality that a poet's words bestow upon the poet who wrote them. Solomon's "Song of Songs" possesses a passion and an eroticism that is timeless. And what of William Shakespeare? All we know of Shakespeare historically is the rather thin biography that scholars have given us. But in his thirty-seven plays, his superb sonnets and the additional poems we have Shakespeare in full, sometimes in the characters of his plays and at other times directly. If we did not have the plays and the poetry, Shakespeare would be just a name parenthesized between 1564 and 1616. But his words survive and transcend the time and place of their creation so that they resonate with people everywhere and at all times. As a matter of personal endorsement of this statement, I knew a foreign author who told me years ago that the only reason he learned English was so that he could read Shakespeare in the original.

During the months when I was preparing to write this essay, I became more and more inclined to the view that power conceived of as force to achieve supremacy or control was in essence related to pride, vanity and egotism. I am not naïve enough to believe that force is not sometimes required in human or national relations. Police work and acts of self defense often justifiably necessitate the use of force. But unless we choose to live in a Hobbesian world where men are regarded as mutually predatory and where power in its most violent forms is seen as the final arbiter, I believe that a more enlightened norm of power should be preferred and extolled. This is the power that I associate with education, love and the liberal and fine arts. The sharing of knowledge has a beneficial effect upon both the teacher and the taught, and its ultimate benefits are incalculable. The power of love—fraternal, conjugal or communal—is at heart the mother and father of trust without which social life is impossible. And finally the liberal and fine arts "enable" men to fulfill their personal and creative natures in ways that simply do not die. Contrasted with power that possesses these attributes, power that is allied with militarism, money, class, race or science, however triumphant it may appear and however long it may prevail, is by nature finite and secondary.

2009

24

EXIT MIRTH, MISDEEDS AND MEMORY

HAVE YOU NOTICED? Little by little over the past ten years we've lost much of our mirth. We've had more than our share of political satire and the endless routines of one stand-up straight man after another, to be sure, but not real mirth. Wit and humor have had little place in general conversation and even less in what has passed for political discourse and dialogue.

This spiritual "downsizing" has been the legacy of the national mood created by the shrunken prune of the fundamentalist mind in cahoots with corporate predators and the neo-conservative fascist way of doing things. Now, to no one's amazement, it seems that the creators of this wasteland are walking away scot-free. There have been some protests, such as that from a steering committee chaired by Dean Lawrence Velvel of the University of Massachusetts Law School and formed for the express purpose of prosecuting "Bush, Vice President Cheney and others." The rationale for prosecution was that "the future could be threatened by additional examples of Executive lawlessness by leaders who need fear no personal consequences for their actions, including more illegal wars like Iraq." There were similar protests from journalists like Nobel awardee Paul Krugman and politicians like Elizabeth Holtzman, but there was also a counterforce urging us to get on with business as usual, turn the page and leave the violators to their millions. We gave lip service to the axiom that no one is above the law and let it go at that. But in the meanwhile a more insidious category was created. Under this category certain malefactors were placed *beyond* the law.

There is ample precedent for this. Richard ("If the President does it, it's not illegal") Nixon was pardoned by Gerald Ford to spare the country the "agony of a trial." Let's put aside for the sake of argument that more than half of the 58,000 Americans killed in Vietnam died after Nixon took office in 1968 on the pledge to end the war. Put aside his "incursion" into Cambodia ("Bomb the bastards") as well as Nelson Rockefeller's insight into Nixon's "peevishness" and historian Richard Hofstadter's linking Nixon to what Hofstadter called the "paranoid style in American politics." That leaves Watergate. Watergate alone as exposed by Robert Woodward and Carl Bernstein and adjudicated by Judge John Sirica was a direct assault on constitutional government, which is as close to "high crimes and misdemeanors" as even the most devoted of Nixon's admirers would have to concede. But in light of Ford's pardon, justice was never served. Nixon's underlings were sentenced for what Nixon orchestrated and approved while Nixon remained *beyond* the law.

Then there was the example of Lieutenant Colonel Oliver North, USMC. Testifying before the Senate under oath in the uniform of a Marine officer, North lied about the Iran-Contra deal, in which money from Iran was diverted to the Contras on Nicaragua. The entire scheme bypassed the Boland Amendment as well as Congressional approval and oversight and created a precedent that led Reagan, who claimed to know nothing of the matter, to fire North. After his trial, an Appeals Court reversed North's three convictions and commuted his three-year sentence. Suddenly finding himself *beyond* the law, North ran for a Senate seat from Virginia, lost a close election to Chuck Robb and moved on to hosting television programs on Fox news devoted to military heroes and giving speeches for fat fees to evangelical audiences. The higher-ups who approved of North's actions—Admiral John Poindexter, Eliot Abrams and Caspar Weinberger—were duly pardoned by President George H. W. Bush. Placed *beyond* the law, Abrams went on to influence Middle East policies in the administration of Bush *fils,* despite the fact that Abrams' biases in the area were widely known. It seems that when a man is *beyond* the law a la Abrams, he is also beyond disqualification.

The list goes on. There was Marc Rich, a contributor to the Democratic party, who was indicted for chicanery *in absentia* and pardoned by President Clinton as a favor to Prime Minister Ehud Barak. Then there is Lewis Libby, who treasonously exposed the identity of CIA agent Valerie Plame and placed her very life in jeopardy by doing so. To the consternation of his Conservative allies, he had his sentence for this crime commuted and permanently suspended by George W. Bush in lieu of a widely expected pardon. Regardless, in fact if not in name Libby received a semi-pardon that put him *beyond* the law.

This same spirit of exoneration can be applied to the former President himself. Here was a man who with a stroke of the pen legitimized preventive war (essentially approving war by executive choice), authorized torture in Abu Ghraibs (plural!), wiretapped and eaves-dropped at will, made "rendition" a household word, installed groupthink and ventriloquism as hallmarks of his entire administration and, along with Condoleezza Rice, blocked by America's veto the otherwise unanimously UN-ordered cease-fire in Lebanon and later in Gaza, both of which have been cited by various groups as examples where war was deliberately waged against civilian populations as a criminal form of collective punishment.

Overlooking the characterizations of Bush by Will Ferrell and his counterpart on Saturday Night Live, we have in point of fact a man who assumed that he received orders from God, that he was a single force against evil (reminiscent of Melville's Ahab, who took upon himself to rid the world of the white whale of evil and was in due course destroyed by it) and that those who were not with him were against him. (In his recently published THE IRONY OF MANIFEST DESTINY William Pfaff has noted that Bush tried unsuccessfully to enlist Jacques Chirac's support for the war in Iraq by telling him that the removal of Saddam Hussein would be a preface to the rapture, the Second Coming and other such folderol.) In this he is a perfect replica of a character named Holy Willie in the poetry of Robert Burns. Burns portrays Holy Willie as someone who is totally blameless by his own standards, blames others for his and the world's problems, is merciful to those who agree with him and merciless to those who do not and is scornful of the opinion of others.

Though Jefferson urged leaders to have a decent respect for the opinions of mankind, Bush ignored the protests of 10,000,000 here and throughout the world before he visited "shock and awe" on the Iraqis. He not only was convinced that he was *beyond* the law but that he was law unto himself. When President Obama was still a state official and protested the war that Bush was about to unleash on Iraq as illegal and unnecessary, he eerily and ironically echoed Lincoln's criticism of President Polk's war with Mexico—a war that Lincoln considered unjust as its core even though it was championed by American "patriots" who believed in American expansionism regardless of the cost in lives or treasure. Polk stuck with his decision (sound familiar?). Lincoln then accused Polk of exceeding executive power and ignoring Congress (sound familiar?), of misusing language and shuffling the facts (sound familiar?) and of manipulating public opinion by lies of commission and omission. In an attempt to rationalize what he had initiated, Bush in one of his final statements as President said that some might question his original decision but no one could question the results. If we put aside how pretentious this statement really is (are the so-called "results" anything to brag about: a charade of an election, the selection of a Prime Minister of our choosing after the elected Prime Minister was found wanting, the pay-offs to tribal chiefs to keep them servile, the recurrent car-bombs in crowded areas?), the logic of it is self-incriminating.

If the original decision was in the very least "questionable" and if the result of that decision plunged the country into war on one-man's say-so, the focus should be on the morality of the original decisions regardless of the results. Otherwise, it sounds like an argument of the ends justifying the means, and there's not moralist on earth who would accept that. President Obama's non-repudiation and extension of Bush's policies and even his own decision to "democratize" Afghanistan now make a mockery of his pre-Presidential positions.

As reprehensible as it is to have individuals placed *beyond* the law by whatever justification, the results naturally are more catastrophic when this same exemption is applied to or assumed by nations. From the time George W. Bush gave Ariel Sharon *carte blanche* to work his will against the Palestinians, the Israelis have been able to act unilaterally without any second thoughts about world opinion or action as long as the United States had the power of the veto in the United Nations. This in effect has placed them *beyond* the law. If they chose to put up a wall that encroached on land that was not theirs, the wall went up, and Americans footed the bill. If it sundered families and obstructed travel or trips to and from school or employment, so be it. If being stopped at an Israeli checkpoint resulted in the death of someone needing medical attention or in the protracted anguish of a woman in labor, so be it. If protests against such practices came from the Red Cross, Red Crescent or United Nations officials in the territories, they could be ignored with impunity because they could not be enforced upon a government that considered itself *beyond* such laws or stipulations.

The invasion of Lebanon in 2006 was said to have been provoked by a border incident that resulted in the death of Israeli soldiers and the capture of two Israeli soldiers by Hezbollah. In fact, such border clashes were not uncommon, but the Israelis seized upon this one to put into action a plan that had been in place for months. (Apparently, the release from captivity of the two Israeli soldiers was not the primary concern; after all the destruction that was visited upon Lebanon, the soldiers are still prisoners.) The purpose of the attack was to crush Hezbollah. To that end the Israelis generalized the attack, targeting villages in the south and in Beirut itself where Shiites were in a majority and then spreading destruction throughout the country in the hope that the Lebanese would blame Hezbollah and turn against it. After the third day of the war every country in the world except the United States, Great Britain and Israel voted for the attack to end. The attack went on, courtesy of George W. Bush and the compliant Tony Blair. More than 1,000 Lebanese killed, an uncounted number wounded, and 150,000 displaced. Bridges were destroyed, the airport immobilized, electrical plants hit and an oil facility bombed so that an oil spill pollutes to this day the beaches in Lebanon, Syria, Turkey and Greece. In addition, the Israelis targeted buildings in the south of Lebanon, including a school in Qana where one hundred children were killed. The Israelis claimed that the school was a Hezbelloh hideout, that the children were used as shields and so on and so on. Evidence after the war contradicted such claims. In a memorable footnote to that period, Condoleezza Rice was flying from Israel to Beirut after a cease-fire had finally taken hold. Looking at Beirut from the air, she pronounced it "The birth of the new Middle East." As if such astigmatism were not insult enough, the Lebanese had a groundlevel view of the death and destruction that Dr. Rice had insouciantly permitted to happen. Politely the Lebanese told her not to land.

The subsequent onslaught in Gaza was but a variation on the same theme. Again, President Bush and the Israel leaders ignored the protests of millions throughout the world. It was true that rockets from Hamas forces of Gaza were falling in southern Israel. What was also true was that the so-called cease-fire was originally broken by Israel's continuing blockade and choking control of points of entry and egress from Gaza. This does not justify the indiscriminate rocket attacks (nothing does), but it goes a long way in explaining them. In the open prison or ghetto that the Israelis made of Gaza, the effect on the Gazans was equivalent to suffocation. Someone compared it to being trapped in a dark and crowded elevator underground. The impression was that anyone so trapped would stop at nothing to be free. (The Israeli policy of strangulation was recently compounded by the interdiction of a peace flotilla in international waters, the killing of nine passengers on one of the ships and a propaganda barrage to the effect that "thugs" were aboard one of the ships and "ready to fight." All of this wearisome repetition of history had as its scarcely disguised purpose the attempt to discredit Hamas in the eyes of the Gazans.)

Analogies aside, the Israeli attacks in 2009 from the air, sea and ground were permitted to go on for approximately three weeks. The death count was thirteen Israelis killed compared to over one thousand four hundred Gazans, more than eight hundred of whom were children and women. The imposed misery on the Gazans has prompted many to identify what happened and what is happening as a humanitarian catastrophe. Such are the facts. Again, the pretexts were a re-hash of what was said in Lebanon. Punished so ruthlessly, the Gazans would blame Hamas and turn against it, or so the Israelis believed. They also said that the deaths of so many innocents was the fault of Hamas, who used women and children as shields and so on and so on. *No one bothered to give the counterargument, namely, if Hamas knew in advance that the Israelis would attack civilians, why would they be so stupid as to be in the same vicinity as civilians?* The more realistic view of the entire war was that it was meant to be as punitive as possible and that the Israeli government was using the pretext of having Hamas blamed for breaking the cease-fire when in fact the charge was totally false. If any side was responsible for breaking the non-existent cease-fire, it was the Israelis. But don't take my word for it. Here is what Uri Avinery, one of Israel's most distinguished journalists, wrote in HAARETZ: "As a matter of fact, the cease-fire did not collapse, because there was no cease-fire to begin with. The main argument for any cease-fire in the Gaza Strip must be the opening of border crossings. There can be no life in Gaza without a steady flow of supplies. But the crossings were not opened, except for a few hours now and again. The blockade on land, on sea and in the air against a million and a half human beings is an act of war, as much as any dropping of bombs or launching of rockets. It paralyzes life in the Gaza Strip: eliminating most sources of employment, pushing hundreds of thousands to the brink of starvation, stopping most hospitals from functioning, disrupting the supply of electricity and water...Then there came small provocations which were designed to get Hamas to act. After several months in which hardly any Qassam rockets were launched, an army unit was sent into the Strip…the aim was to find a pretext for the termination of the cease-fire, in a way that made it plausible to blame the Palestinians. And indeed, after several such small actions, in which Hamas fighters were killed, Hamas retaliated with a massive launch of rockets, and…the cease-fire was at an end. Everybody blamed Hamas."

Roger Cohen in his recently published "Eyeless in Gaza" confirms Avinery's analysis: "Long before the six-month cease-fire crumbled in mid-December (a little over a month after the November 4 Israeli raid into Gaza that killed six Hamas militants), Israel has also cut delivery of critical supplies of food, medicine, fuel, fertilizer, cash and spare parts to a trickle."

Creating desperate conditions, though it may not justify how those made desperate might act in reprisal, does at the very least explain why the desperate may have acted as they did. In fact this played into the hands of those Israelis who were simply waiting for a reason to invade Gaza, and the rest is history. With self-defense as its justification the Israeli forces attacked Gaza as a whole for almost a month—a period made possible by the non-action of the United States to compel a cessation. Israel acted within that period as a nation *beyond* the law. For Roger Cohen the result was not a victory in any sense of the word: "Israel, backed by the United States, has been intent on proving that Hamas must wither and die rather than exploring ways in which it, like the Palestine Liberation Organization before it, can move toward being part of a two-state solution. That is a strategic mistake. Hamas, even with perhaps three hundred of its leaders and militants killed, has been strengthened as a political and social movement by Olmert's last fling, the reckless foray of a failed leader."

As prescient as Mr. Cohen's remarks are, they ignore an uglier truth that is probably at the heart of the attitude of various Israeli governments toward the Palestinians. It was frankly stated by Arnon Soffer, one of Sharon's advisors on demography: "When 1.5 million people live in a closed-off Gaza, it's going to be a human catastrophe. Those people will become even bigger animals than they are today with the aid of an insane fundamentalist Islam. The pressure at the border will be awful. It's going to be a terrible war. So, if we want to remain alive, we will have to kill and kill and kill. All day, every day." With such a mindset it is only logical that the Israelis would use the full range of their arsenal plus white phosphorus against the population in the same way they used their ordnance plus a million cluster bomblets in southern Lebanon.

It is important to note here that Mr. Soffer's proclamation is offensive to a growing number of Israelis and to American Jews. Among the most prominent Israelis and American Jews in opposition to the Likud-Netanyahu view of things are Daniel Barenboim (Israel's leading composer and symphonic conductor), David Grossman and Amoz Oz (two of Israel's best novelists), Israeli journalists Uri Avinery and Gideon Levy, members of the Peace Now movement, Howard Zinn (the American historian), Tony Judt, Naom Chomsky, Richard Falk (Professor Emeritus from Princeton and head of the U. N. Commission on Human Rights) and the aforementioned Roger Cohen. These individuals are in the same tradition as the Nobelist Harold Pinter, Albert Einstein, Tanya Rinehart, Martin Buber, Arthur Miller, Richard Dreyfuss and even Abba Eban in his later years. They were not in the majority. Dissenters rarely are. But they personified the truths of Judaism that will outlast those who consider themselves *beyond* the law in the affairs of nations as well as those journalists and others who support them, i.e., Krauthammer, Frum, Brooks, Kristol, Foxman, Perle and Dershowitz.

Identifying individuals or governments as wrongdoers for whom law has little or no power of restraint is not fingerpointing. It is in the Judaic tradition of rendering just judgment. Avoiding such judgments is a disservice to history. Provided that such judgments are not made in the spirit of revenge or retribution, they can truly show past acts for what they were and serve as warnings against their recurrence in the future. What's needed is to put the blame or the guilt with those who consider themselves *beyond* the law. That's justice. Until such justice is in some way courageously served, our mirth will probably remain dormant.

2010

25

FULL-TIME FAIRNESS FOR PART-TIME HELP

MOST OBSERVERS would agree that many universities today are little more than academic corporations that no longer champion liberal education before bequeathing to their graduates a "degree in debt." Such debts often reach six figures and require a lifetime to remit while the lenders, private or governmental, receive millions in interest and enrich themselves tenfold.

It's been said that we often accept what we choose to get used to. Sadly, we have chosen to get used to the corporate university with its rising tuition costs, which are passed on in true business fashion to the consumers (students and their parents). How many families can afford tuition/room/board costs that run from $40,000 to $68,000 per year nationally—and rising? Unless we favor education only for the ultra-wealthy or affluent, the answer is that only few can without extensive borrowing. Anyone with sense knows that this cannot go on.

The effect this has on students is predictable. They will be drawn to technological and related programs (job training actually) that seem to promise sure employment upon graduation so that they can begin to replay their loans. (This in itself is a myth since the constant change in technologies often makes such careful preparations redundant). They will have to defer marriage and home purchases. The effect on "accommodating" universities is that the ideal of the liberally educated student (he or she who is primarily concerned with learning how to live rather than how to make a living) will become secondary.

It seems only logical to me that universities—in order to avoid the corporate drift to bottom-line thinking—should be even more devoted to liberal education and strengthening their faculties accordingly. The recent trend toward hiring adjunct teachers and professors, however competent they may be, to "remedy" the situation is often just a way of saving and accruing money for the university, i.e. profiteering.

An adjunct is by definition one who is employed when the regular faculty is overburdened and needs supplementary help on a part-time basis. Or an adjunct is someone hired to provide special skills for a contracted period. Adjuncts are not meant to be hired en masse because the administration balks at hiring additional full-time regular faculty to meet scheduling needs. Notre Dame, for example, rejected that option when the faculty voted that adjuncts could never exceed 25% of the faculty, and in practice the number is much less than that.

Currently at Duquesne University, where the number of adjuncts exceeds that of the regular faculty, an adjunct in the College of Liberal Arts is paid $4,000 per semester to teach a three-credit course. The cost to the student for such a course is approximately $3,000. Assume for the moment that thirty students enroll in the course. This means that the university derives $90,000 from that course alone. Deducting the adjunct's fee of $4,000 from the total sum leaves the university with $86,000. The adjunct receives no health or retirement benefits whatsoever since these are reserved for full-time faculty members.

I discovered that there are now roughly 500 adjunct teachers and professors at Duquesne University, where I taught for forty-three years. (In the past few years the number has varied between 486 and 513). If you apply the same mathematical calculations to this number as I applied to a single adjunct, the results are astounding. If each of the almost 500 adjuncts university-wide teaches but a single class at the aforementioned pay of $4,000 per class, the total income to the university per semester ($90,000 multiplied by 500) is $45,000,000. The total cost for adjuncts ($4,000 multiplied by 500) is $2,000,000. Deducting the adjuncts' total costs from the total income to the university still leaves the university a net income of $43,000,000 per semester. Even if the enrollment per class were fifteen instead of thirty, the difference between tuition income—less adjunct costs—would still leave the university with an aggregate income per semester of $20,500,000. To derive any pleasure from the fact that this net income is anything but a profit created by the use of adjuncts rather than regular faculty (no matter how it may be praised by the Dougherty administration inured to profit-and-loss audits) strikes me as specious in the extreme. This may be just business as usual for Walmart or McDonald's, but should it be for a university? Is this where "higher" education is heading?

The decision by the adjuncts in the College to unionize in affiliation with the United Steelworkers of America should hardly be surprising, particularly, as stated by Duquesne alumna Eileen Colianni, when 25% of the adjuncts nation-wide have to rely on public assistance to make ends meet. The goal is obviously to enable the adjuncts to bargain for a more equitable payment in relation to the income received and also to have medical, pharmaceutical and retirement benefits that every employee needs. If collective bargaining and affiliation with the USW is the best way to achieve these goals, why is there any resistance?

The argument has been raised by the Duquesne administration that its status as a religious institution exempts it from rulings of the National Labor Relations Board. When Georgetown University was confronted by the efforts of adjuncts to unionize, it not only refused to claim such an exemption but welcomed the effort. Georgetown's Provost, Dr. Robert M. Grove, stated at the time: "We are pleased to inform you that Georgetown and SEIU Local 500 have reached tentative agreement on all of the terms of the first collective bargaining agreement covering part-time faculty at the Main Campus… We are hopeful that, through this agreement, and through our continued work together, part-time faculty members in our community will feel as welcome and valued as other faculty members."

Such a spirit of colleague-to-colleague candor is certainly more welcome than a protracted and needless rivalry, particularly in light of the income derived from adjunct labor in relation to the profit to the university. Georgetown is certainly no less a Catholic university than Duquesne. Although one Duquesne administrator, whose opinion I respect, stated that the university's attitude toward its adjuncts has always been one of consideration and concern, this is not the real issue. Benevolence is no substitute for justice, and justice is the only issue here. Why should the adjuncts accept a situation that they choose not to get used to? And why should the university accept a situation that an equally prestigious university in the nation's capital chose, to its credit, not to get used to? If magnanimity remains a Christian virtue, the answer is obvious.

2015

26

NO SPACE LIKE HOME

In 1999 I returned to Notre Dame for the fifty-year reunion of the class of 1949. I had missed all previous class reunions for various reasons, but I decided it was important to come to this one. I might add that my wife, whose ardor for Notre Dame is second to none, may have had something to do with that.

A month or so before the event my friend and classmate Joe O'Brien, who is also the class secretary, called and asked me if I would consider writing a poem to celebrate the occasion. I told Joe that poems "written for occasions" were rarely worth anything and that, although I appreciated his asking me, I thought it was not a good idea.

As the date neared, I was startled out of sleep one night by a dream too relevant to be ignored. In this dream the reunion had already happened, and I had indeed written a poem that I dreamt I quoted at the farewell dinner. In fact, the poem in the dream stayed with me as I woke—not totally but in parts—, and I wrote as much as I could remember of it on a sheet of paper. All that day I worked on my memory of that poem until I finished it. I waited several days to see if it would still "hold up." Finally, I called Joe and told him that the poem I had written regarded the reunion as already behind us, but that he was welcome to it if he thought it appropriate.

We've journeyed back to grass
  and souvenirs and beige bricks.
The sky's exactly the same.
Acre by acre the campus
  widens like a stage designed
  for a new play.
              Why
  do we gawk like foreigners
  at residence halls no longer
  ours but somehow ours
  in perpetuity?
              We visit them
  like their alumni—older
  but unchanged.
                Half a century
  of students intervenes.
                  They stroll
  among us now, invisible
  but present as the air before
  they fade and disappear.
                   It's like
  the day we swam St. Joseph's
  Lake.
        We churned the surface
  into suds with every stroke and kick.
After we crossed, the water
  stilled and settled to a sheen
  as if we never swam at all.

One memory was all we kept
to prove we'd been together
in that very lake, and swimming.
Each time we tell this story,
someone says we're living out
a dream.
We say we're only
reuniting with the lives
we lived.
As long as we
can say they were, they were…
And what they were, we are.

Looking back on that reunion experience (as it actually was as well as how I imagined it would be) has made me regard returns of this kind as more than mere nostalgia. I've come to the conclusion that they are related to one of the deepest compulsions in each of us, and that is the drama of leaving "home" and then coming back. Subconsciously many of us at the 1999 reunion felt that we were in a sense "coming home." For a number of our undergraduate years Notre Dame had been a *home* to us. Of course, it was never fully "home" because as students we invariably counted the days until we could return during Christmas or mid-term breaks to Pittsburgh, Boston, Kalamazoo, Birmingham, Phoenix or wherever. A home away from home, however dear it may historically or actually be, is not quite the same as home.

The experience of leaving home for college, war, work or diversion is now commonplace. The leaving may be difficult or perfunctory or routine. If you know you're leaving (or have to leave) permanently, it's painful. If it's anything less, you look forward to coming back. Coming back from war, for example, to be reunited with loved ones is a joy beyond words. Coming back from work makes a person realize what he is actually working for. And returning from a vacation or a stint in college rewards us with a sense of familiarity as we survey rooms that seem to have been waiting for us. No matter what the reason is that we leave or have to leave home, we look forward to returning for only one reason—to be in that space where we are at home. There is simply no substitute for it.

In literature we find the theme of departure and return in everything from Homer's ODYSSEY to the parable of the prodigal son to Alfred Lord Tennyson's ENOCH ARDEN to the adventures of Robinson Crusoe to the saga of Huckleberry Finn. I even see it in the game of baseball. Having played it when younger and being a lifelong devotee, I know it in my genes that a batter comes to home plate with the hope of returning to home plate again. In short, he not only does not want to make an out, but he wants to score. If he hits a home run, the circling of the bases is a mere formality. By scoring, he is fulfilled as a batter; he's lived the purpose of the game. If his homer is a game-winner, he is greeted by his team mates at home plate like a conquering hero with backslaps, tussles, high-fives and the entire chromatic scale of praise. If he hits a single, double or a triple, he must rely on other batters to get him to home plate. Being stranded at first, second or third is non-fulfilling because the return to home plate has been denied. Getting home, in the parlance of the game, is all that counts. Literally.

Recently the importance of home to one man made a lasting impression on me when I read the late Anthony Shadid's

HOUSE OF STONE. Shadid, the winner of two Pulitzer Prizes for reportage, was the chief Middle East correspondent for the NEW YORK TIMES. He covered the wars in Iraq, Libya and Syria. It was while leaving Syria in a horse convoy (because road travel was too perilous) that Shadid died of a severe asthmatic attack. It was discovered after his death that he was mortally allergic to horses. But prior to that he had decided to take a year off from his posts in Iraq and Libya and, rather than return to his home in Washington or to his native Oklahoma, he thought that it would be resuscitating to re-build and restore the stone house of his grandparents in Marjayoun, Lebanon. With the help of a motley crew of stonemasons and other craftsmen, he did just that although his death in Syria prevented him from seeing the job completed. But, as he narrates in HOUSE OF STONE, it was his connection with the Shadid family's ancestral home that saved him from a depression to which he was prone after witnessing the horrific effects of war on the populations in Iraq, Libya and, finally, Syria. For Shadid the idea of home—or rather the restoration of a home—restored him as well. His family, realizing that, decided justly that he should be buried in Marjayoun.

The prize-winning memoirist N. Scott Momaday once wrote that a man in his lifetime once "ought to give himself to a particular landscape in his experience, to look at it from as many angles as he can, to wonder upon it, to dwell upon it." It lately has become apparent to me that for many years I have looked at the city of Pittsburgh in just this spirit. Born, bred and "buttered" here, I feel essentially alien when I am away from it for too long, no matter where I am. Even in the south of France, which has the climate, the pace, the cuisine and the Mediterranean blend of work and leisure that attract me as nothing else can, I reach a point while I am there when I simply want to come home in order to feel "at home." This puts me at odds with one Czech writer who claimed that a man is not fully human until he achieves a state of being resident nowhere, thus truly becoming a citizen of the world. And it leaves me diametrically opposed to the great Argentinian writer and dissident Jacobo Timmerman after he was persecuted and exiled by the military junta. In exile Timmerman stated: "I am more at home in subjects now, not countries." In my defense I cannot help but note that these comments were made by men who actually were refugees and that such statements could readily be seen as the fall-back credos of men forced into permanent exile. I even have the feeling that the statements smack of rationalization, and understandably so.

A person's addresses and orientations may change, but the fact of the matter is that no one is from everywhere. Each of us is from somewhere, and if that somewhere remains accessible to us and we live there by choice, then to call it anything else but home is plain wrong. Being from a particular somewhere we draw a certain strength from and feel the pride of loyalty to our residence there. We are part of the whole.

When asked why I have stayed and continue to stay in Pittsburgh, I never can give a specific reason. It's like being asked why my wife and I chose one another or why I do what I do. The answer gets bogged down in the mystery of life itself. Eventually I wonder if I actually did the choosing or, vocationally speaking, was chosen. When pressed, I give the usual reasons, i.e., it's where I earn my living, where my family has been and still is, where my friends (and enemies) of longstanding still are, where I like the change of seasons and so on. But I know in my heart that these are not the reasons as much as they are simply facts. I suspect that I live in Pittsburgh because I have never discovered or felt the need of another home anywhere else. True, history and upbringing and happenstance all had something to do with my staying. But there was and always is something more. I sense this each time I visit the plot of graves in Calvary Cemetery in the city where the deceased members of my family are buried. While I am there, I understand what continuity means. It's what the living always feel when they are in the presence of the graves of those once loved…and still loved. Beyond religious belief, beyond the ineluctable ties of blood, beyond all power but the power of love itself, I know that the remains of those who raised me are there beneath my feet, and in the grip of feelings generated by that remembrance I have shamelessly knelt and prayed on that grave-cluttered slope for these dear and definite few. In a larger sense it's as if America exists in miniature in the ten or fifteen square yards of Pennsylvania that holds them. It confers on the city that was their home and that has been and still is mine more than a geographical importance. It makes it mine; it literally becomes me, a part of me forever.

This might even explain a phenomenon for which Pittsburgh has become widely and uniquely known. It's a matter of historical fact that the city's population has dwindled from more than 600,000 in the 1950's and 1960's to roughly 360,000 now. The young began looking elsewhere for their lives, while the older grew older and died. This was true even though the city was and still is known internationally for its medical facilities, its universities and its diversified light and heavy industries. But what emerges as a matter of amazement is that many of the departees who left in their twenties and thirties came back when they were in their sixties and seventies. Many even moved into some of the very houses and neighborhoods where they were raised to live out their retirements. For this reason Allegheny County has the second highest percentage of senior residents in the entire country. (The first unsurprisingly is a county in Florida.) If this return "exodus" is not a testimony to the magnetic pull of "home," I have no other way of explaining it.

During my visits to Notre Dame in the past few decades, I realized that what was a home away from home for me and many other alumni was truly a home for the priests, brothers and some of the resident lay teachers who gave their very lives to their work at the university. They are buried in the Holy Cross Cemetery. On one return visit I decided quite spontaneously to take a walk through the cemetery, stopping here and there when I recognized a name. A poem actually came of it.

So many gone to graves
 and all in regimental order…
Headstoned by squat crosses
 and ranked in death's exact
 chronology, they answer
 to the names we had for them:
 "Black Mac" McCarragher,
 Leo "Rational" Ward,
 "Big" and "Little" McAvoy,

Boarman the orator, and Eugene
Burke of the pinched pince-nez.
To see their lives reduced
to digits on a cross seems almost
disrespectful.
Sameness they hated
to a man, but now they're stuck
with it.
And yet there's something
just in this most orderly
democracy.
Each man is buried
minutes from the work that was
his life.
Together they resemble
soldiers buried by battalions
near their battlefields.
Here's Kehoe
the Prefect.
Here's tall and scholarly
Soleta.
Here's Frank the fiery
centaur of the lot.
A trio
of fresh, white tulips decorates
the plot that claimed him forty
years ago.
Who put them there?

Thoughts that prompt a poem like this invariably raise important, existential questions. Paul Gauguin grouped them succinctly as the title of one of his most memorable paintings: "Who are we? Where do we come from? Where are we going?" All spiritual quests and all religions address themselves ultimately to these questions. The answers depend on the faith of the questioner, who hopes that his faith will be rewarded. It could be reunion with Christ, with God, with holiness itself, with family and loved ones, with the spirit of the universe. The answer is never a matter of absolute knowledge but a matter of faith. And the answer is unknowable this side of death as much as we would like it to be. We simply live in hope, which for Christians is the crucial virtue that unites faith and charity. It's the one virtue that impels us to live, regardless.

I think that the homing instinct in each of us carries over into the sense that life itself could be something similar to a journey home. Many writers have described an afterlife in these terms. They all reflect the view that the homing instinct seems too deep and universal to be confined to our "ground time" in the here and now. They imply that it could be a foretelling. We shall see.

2000-2005

27

O SAY CAN'T YOU SEE

LATELY I'VE BEEN ITEMIZING how America has changed for the worst over the past four decades. Some will disagree with what I have concluded. Some might be offended while some might concur, albeit quietly. My only fallback will be to let the facts speak for themselves.

Now that we are in an election year, the negatives in our political life are too obvious to ignore. Dominated by advertising in the media, as well as the mail, the telephone and the internet, we are flooded with vapid commercials. Subtlety has long since left the building. Debates between candidates, as Arthur Miller wrote in ON POLITICS AND THE ART OF ACTING, are little more than stage shows. Political rallies are star-spangled outlets for noise. The poet and critic Louis Simpson has written that the very act of voting has become as perfunctory as going to the bathroom, a necessity for a decreasing number of voters to be done as quickly as possible. More about this later...

Then there is what passes for the media, much of it corporately owned and controlled. In newspapers the reports of bombings, murders and crashes rule the telegrammic headlines while lesser catastrophes fill the inner pages in descending order of importance. Newscasters or radio and television anchors invariably speak in the key of alarm, and the programming is scaled, as in the print media, from major to lesser disasters to conclude with some account of human interest ("The family dog awakened a sleeping family to a fire in the basement of their home..."} at the conclusion. It's all entwined with commercials timed to the attention span of the passive.

Then there is the lucrative and expanding presence of drugs, performance-enhancing and otherwise, at all levels of American society. A few years ago I was invited to speak at the convention of plastic surgeons. Also on the program was a nationally known surgeon who addressed himself to the dangers of snorting cocaine. He said there were only two possible consequences. The first was death, and he corroborated this by alluding to the death of a famous basketball player who died on the court after snorting cocaine for the first time before a game. The second result was the gradual erosion of nasal bone tissue and the sinuses below and above the eyes. In this connection he described his treatment of a young female addict whose nose had literally collapsed and flattened on her face. He helped her surgically but warned her that such surgery had no second act. After the program concluded, I asked him why such knowledge about death or disfigurement from cocaine use was not more widely known to the public. He simply shrugged.

Another regression is the overwhelming exhibitionism and exaggeration in public behavior, especially in sports. I refer to the end-zone behavior of players after scoring a touchdown.

They perform a minuet or else squat, somersault or wait to be embraced or mobbed by anyone in sight.

So many of these weaknesses in our national character often find their moment to coalesce and show us what we have become. The vaudevillian catfight now masquerading as a presidential election may be such a moment. It has prompted many to ask, "How did we get to this point?" Perhaps the best way to address (if not answer) this question is to consider, not only the regressions I have already listed, but what our country has become in the last fifty or so years.

First, the effects of war. Since the end of Word War II but particularly since 1965, we have become inured to the daily death counts and casualty lists created by war. The approximate total number of American war-deaths from 1965 to the present is 66,000. The wounded along with civilian deaths reach a much higher number. Meanwhile those in the population of Vietnam, Afghanistan and Iraq that we have killed is over one million. This has prompted some historians to claim that we have killed more people in the last fifty or so years than any other nation. The irony is that these presidentially chosen wars have now been shown to have had no legal or moral justification. Nothing reveals this more succinctly than George W. Bush's answer to Richard B. Clark, Chairman of the Counterterrorism Group, when Clark questioned the legality of the invasion of Iraq that Bush was determined to launch. "I don't care what the international lawyers say," Bush bragged, "we are going to kick some a—." So began the ongoing deterioration of the Middle East on orders from a former collegiate cheerleader. That seems blameworthy enough but even more blameworthy are those who never charged Bush judicially with taking the country to war unjustifiably. Lyndon Johnson benefitted from the same legal disregard over his hyping the war in Vietnam for cooked-up reasons.

One result of this is that we have become a people inured to indifference to the law by elected officials while simply accepting the reverberating effects that such indifference has on other aspects of our very lives. I often wonder if our resignation to military deaths is related to our acceptance of homicides at home–approximately 80 per day. I wonder also if the military's reliance on force as a problem-solver is related to the self-arming of the population. At this writing the number of guns in the country outnumbers the census—300,000,000 plus.

The effect of war on the outlook of citizens has been accompanied by a change in demographics since what Arthur Miller called the "Reagan trance." In the 1980's the wealthy constituted about 10% of the population. By the end of the Reagan administration that figure was close to doubling while the Lower Middle Class (and poor) increased from 20% to 30%. In terms of arithmetic this means that the Middle Class had shrunk... and the Middle Class is America at work.

What were the results? One of the results was that young men unable to find work were joining the military as a viable option with its promise of the G. I. Bill and sizable bonuses for extension. This in turn enriched the pool of servicemen to be committed to another presidentially chosen war. The Pentagon, which has a larger public relations budget than any comparable government or fiscal institution on the face of the earth, cooperated with incentive advertising and other inducements to enlistment and extension. The reality is that an all-volunteer military assures compliance without dissent. The dark side to this is that repeated deployments in dangerous areas might have a connection to the number of suicides of men on active duty (some 300 per year). Among veterans (including Iraq and Afghanistan veterans) the rate is more than 20 per day.

For young people not involved in the military, the most desirable option is a college education. With room, board and tuition running annually at some universities to more than $65,000 plus clothing and travel, only the wealthy or those resigned to a lifetime of debt can cope with collegiate costs. Noam Chomsky even implies that some universities may be heightening costs and becoming more concerned with profit than education. I would like not to believe this, but there is no question that the lenders are profiting and that the student-debtors become more concerned with debt remission than with dissent on public issues. Whether they are complicit or not, the universities may be curbing public dissent on war policies by graduating students whose first concern is debt reduction. It's worth thinking about.

The final contributor to public distrust in government is our tolerance of pressures from foreign governments and domestic lobbyists over American foreign policy. Client nations like Saudi Arabia and Israel are constantly striving to have our interests made identical with their own. The Saudis, where no one without a spermatic link with the governing "royal family" has a real voice, remain displeased over American détente with Iran and our pleas for restraint in Yemen. The Israelis went so far as to collude with Republican political leaders to have Prime

Minister Netanyahu speak to a joint session of Congress in opposition to the Iran issue and other matters. Obama, who had not even been told of the invitation, amazingly said nothing to denounce this open insult to the Presidency itself. But sixty members of Congress proved themselves defiantly offended (as expressed by Congressman Earl Blumenauer of Oregon on You-Tube) by not attending the speech that was greeted by robot-like standings and sittings and applause by the obsequious attendees.

Lately a Las Vegas billionaire named Adelson with a fortune fleeced from suckers at Casino games has pledged $100,000,000 to Trump to influence Middle East policy while his counterpart, a Hollywood producer named Saban, has pledged comparable millions to Hillary Clinton for the same purpose. All such "contributions" are legally sacrosanct now because of the Supreme Court's 5-4 passage of Citizens United, which equates political gifting with free speech so that "money" now literally "talks."

Facing the options, voters are increasingly being urged to choose the lesser evil. This is nothing but a craven escape masquerading as a conscientious alternative. Evil is presented as just another abstract noun. But just suppose the options had to do with relief from constipation, and the sufferer was offered two equally repugnant laxatives and asked to choose. Political constipation is our present condition, and the present "laxatives" being offered do not promise much more than a prolongation, not a cure.

None of the aforementioned pressures on our national life shows signs of vanishing. Neo-con greed is firmly ensconced.

The historian Tony Judt has stated accurately, "We have pursued our self-interest (defined as maximum economic advantage) with minimal reference to extraneous criteria such as altruism, self-denial, taste, cultural habit or collective purpose." The policies of the New Deal and the progressive legislation of the early 1960's were altruistic at the core, and the country as a whole benefitted from Social Security, the G. I. Bill of Rights, Medicare, Medicaid, the Civil Rights Bill, Headstart, Student Loans, the Peace Corps, Food Stamps, the National Endowment for the Arts, the National Endowment for the Humanities and the Corporation for Public Broadcasting. There's been nothing as altruistic since. Since both nominees for the Presidency are viscerally war-hawks and inspire nothing but distaste in more than 50% of the shrinking electorate, the resurrection of such altruism is unlikely.

2016

28

NOT YET OR EVER OVER IT

"GET OVER IT!" That was Ari Fleischer's advice to those dissenters who believed that George W. Bush with the help of Karl Rove and the neo-cons swiped the 2000 presidential election. Fleischer was Bush's press secretary at the time.

If the moral imagination is what enables us to identify chicanery or wrongdoing when it happens and to see where such malfeasance, if not confronted, will lead, the gradual death of the moral imagination in our country began in 2000 for those who agreed to "get over it."

In the years since Fleischer heaped scorn on the disgruntled, I for one have yet to "get over it"—and not exclusively for partisan reasons. Although it will bore those already familiar with the facts as well as those who have opted for historical amnesia, I think it might be enlightening to consider what we were told to get over and what it cost us. Before the vote count was stopped in Florida and the election dumped into the waiting lap of the Supreme Court, the civilian vote-counters had seen Bush's lead over Al Gore reduced from thousands to a few hundred. Moreover, thousands of votes in some predominantly Democratic counties had yet to be counted. Faced with the prospect of loss, lawyers for Bush were flown in Enron jets to Miami to mount legal challenges. Simultaneously, many workers from the offices of Republican congressmen in Washington were shuttled to Miami to clamor, harass and otherwise make difficult the job of the vote-counters. James Baker, the elder Bush's confidant, cautioned against vote-counting "mischief." Although the Florida Supreme Court ordered that the re-count be continued, the United States Supreme Court stopped the recount, went into instant session and, spearheaded by Justices Scalia and Thomas, gave the election to Bush in a 5-4 vote. Justice Breyer in his dissent said that the court would be forever blemished for its intervention.

For those with a moral imagination, the real issue was that the electorate had been made irrelevant. Millions who had voted nationally as well as those Floridians whose votes were not counted might just as well have sat on their hands. The principle of one-man one-vote was shelved, which meant that democracy itself had been shelved. The entire election was decided by one Justice's vote as a historical first.

Some say that Bush was an "empty-suit President" until 9/11, but the morally imaginative might have sensed how a dubiously installed administration would exploit the moment and turn it to its advantage. With the population fearful, Bush "the decider" assumed a certain omnipotence that the Congress (with one dissenting vote) gave him. In turn, Bush, backed by Tony Blair—the Little Lord Fauntleroy in the cast—who prophesied preposterously that we were forty-five minutes away from annihilation, ordered the conquest of Afghanistan, the invasion of Iraq (though 10 million at home and abroad marched in protest) with a loss to date (excluding Afghanistan) of more than 5,000 Americans killed, 32,000 wounded and multiple thousands with mental problems and an ongoing veterans' suicide rate of 22 a day. Other "benefits" were a war-cost of $420,000,000 per day, the institution of torture from on high, extensive spying and surveillance, wire-tapping and so on. And what of more than 600,000 Iraqi civilian casualties with more than 2,000,000 people displaced? If the goal of the invasion behind the souped-up 9/11 attribution was to get Saddam Hussein, why were the Iraqi people made to pay for it?

Those who hoped (and I was one) that Barack Obama would place a check on wanton militarism were encouraged by his anti-war positions during the 2007 campaign but stunned after his election when he upped the number of military in Afghanistan by 30,000. Another stunner was when he said we should look ahead, not back. Those with a moral imagination know that the present is a future that the past makes possible. That bears repeating: *the present is a future that the past makes possible.* To live in the la-la land of presumption and dreams-to-come and ignore history is as ridiculous as it is foolish, and to hear this from a former professor of Constitutional Law was bizarre. If law is built on anything, it is precedent. By ignoring precedent, Obama instantly made Bush, Cheney, Rumsfeld and Wolfowitz unaccountable for their decisions about the war and everything associated with it. Have we learned nothing from history? These individuals conned the country and got away with it. Of course, such hoaxes had occurred before. Think of

President Polk's pre-war, hyped rhetoric that paved the way for our war with Mexico. One definite but outvoted protester was a young Congressman named Abraham Lincoln. Think of Lyndon Johnson's upscaling of the war in Vietnam because of the attack on an American vessel in the Gulf of Tonkin that never happened. Only two senators (Morse and Gruening) voted against Johnson's request, and both were defeated in the next election.

In foreign policy Obama has legalized many of Bush's "signings" related to assassinations (by drone or otherwise) and still has prisoners (some of whom have been cleared) being held and force-fed in Guantanamo. Armies of private contractors at government expense often outnumber American servicemen and women in many areas deemed essential to American interests. And the trumpeted withdrawal from Iraq could hardly be called voluntary when we were asked to leave by the Maliki government after we refused its demand to make Americans subject to Iraqi law for crimes they committed in Iraq.

The Supreme Court ended the decade with another 5-4 ruling to vex the morally imaginative by stating that private, for-profit corporations be accorded the same First Amendment rights as individual citizens. The giving of money for political purposes was in effect equated with free speech. Translation: dollars were the same as words. The phrase "money talks" was now enshrined as a matter of settled law.

I mentioned earlier in this essay that many would be bored by this recapitulation, and I suspect that many others would disagree with my take on what I regard as grave errors with even graver consequences. The problem is that past errors do not remain in the past. They influence and at times even determine present action and attitudes. Recently, for example, I heard a newswoman on radio report the deaths of fifty-five Iraqis in Baghdad from a suicide bombing, the loss of six Marines in a Blackhawk crash in Afghanistan and the amount of the National Lottery Jackpot ($500,000,000 or so) in exactly the same tone of voice. Am I making too much of this by mentioning it? Or is it something that some other office boy would downplay by saying, "Get Over it?"

This slow unraveling of the moral imagination that remains numb when the reporting of civilian and military deaths are bracketed with a lottery jackpot is not an anomaly. We witnessed the same phenomenon during the Vietnam War when the daily death-count appeared in a small rectangle on the front page of newspapers like the baseball scores. Little by little we became inured to our day-to-day ration of fatalities as we succumbed to the dictum that the war would be decided by body-count. Individual deaths disappeared into the gradually increasing sums. This gave rise to protests, to be sure, but that only happened when the numbers turned into thousands. By then it forced the militarists to realize that American wars had to be kept brief and waged with minimal casualties. Years later the Vietnam death totals made Reagan's "petite" war in Grenada as well as the subsequent bombing of Panama negligible by comparison. Who would bother to note if a few hundred Panamanians lost their lives in "surgical" strikes, particularly if it helped to extricate us from the Vietnam syndrome? The same reasoning surfaced again during the limited invasion of Iraq by the elder Bush.

George W. Bush's invasion of Iraq was not the cakewalk it was supposed to be and resulted in years of occupation and ongoing civil strife. This is the real legacy of what was poetically called Operation Iraqi Freedom. Note the choice of words. It was not a war for oil or a fulfillment of Israeli hopes but a war of emancipation. Euphemisms are preferred by militarists in this regard, and the tactic can be traced all the way back to Troy. The Greeks never said that they were attacking Troy for the sake of having greater access to ports and markets beyond the Dardanelles. Instead they were waging war to avenge the seduction of a willingly kidnapped general's wife named Helen. That made the war sound noble, even chivalrous. As long as our invasion of Iraq was made to appear like an American version of *mission civilisatrice*, it seemed to be tolerable. When this turned out not to be true and the resistance to occupation was seen as deep-seated and ongoing, the administration learned the truth of Robespierre's "Nobody trusts a missionary with a gun."

The more the moral imagination degenerates, the more is reason paralyzed. The irrational at that time becomes reasonable as a basis for action. In such an imaginative and moral vacuum, chaos and violence are born. It was Thornton Wilder who noted presciently that "Cruelty is a failure of the imagination." Translated into the language of politics and foreign policy, this eventually confirms the case for force, military or economic, as the first and not the last option.

"Enforcers" are dogmatic in their conviction that their enemies understand nothing but force. Consequently, no action for them is too extreme to bring about the enemy's capitulation or demise. Moral consequences are totally ignored. The Cuban Missile crisis in the sixties, for example, could easily have metastasized into a nuclear disaster if hard-liners like General Lemay, who proudly authorized the massive fire-bombing of Tokyo in World War II, had their way. Had it not been for President Kennedy's rejection of the counsel of his more militant advisors, the confrontation between the Soviet Union and the United States would have had a different ending. Kennedy's moral imagination created the alternative to force.

Much of our current dilemmas in the Middle East derives from a stand-off between the visionaries and the forceful. There are those in the United States and Israel who believe that force—and only force—is the key to supremacy. The fact that this was proved fallacious in Iraq, where we withdrew like a shamed Gulliver, is ignored. The Israeli leadership, which has already walled itself against perceived problems on the ground, remains adamant about the necessity of the use of force— subtly by settlement expansion and overtly by the use of arms. And its supporters in Congress and elsewhere unconditionally support this position. It was on public display a year or so ago when its Prime Minister Benjamin Netanyahu spoke before Congress at the instigation of the Republican leadership. It was reported that members of Congress rose from their seats twenty-eight times to applaud him. I have no way of checking, but my guess is that even Winston Churchill did not receive such an embrace. Loyalists like Charles Krauthammer and George F. Will and others saw this as solidarity. Many like Chris Hedges, Noam Chomsky and Uri Avinery saw it as servility. But it brought into plain view the ongoing Israelization of American foreign policy in the Middle East that perceptive writers like Chris Hedges and Andrew Bacevich have long since warned against and castigated.

But the fact remains, as the French historian Marc Bloch reminds us, that there is no progress unless there is moral progress. If this no longer engages the public mind as an ideal to work toward, the results to come will be similar to what we have experienced to our shame from 2000 to the present day.

2008

29

PROPHETS VERSUS PROFITS

BEFORE HE LEFT OFFICE, President Eisenhower delivered an unignorable speech that has since been praised but ignored in practice. He warned that an alliance between government and the defense industries had created a "military-industrial complex" that was poised to dominate American foreign policy. All of our executive wars since then have validated Eisenhower's prophecy.

Recently Pitt Chancellor Mark Nordenberg delivered an equally prescient warning in a semi-farewell address at the University of Pittsburgh. He stated that the cutting of state funding for higher education, not only in Pennsylvania but nationally, would force a curtailment of innovation and research, eviscerate undergraduate programs and burden students with onerous debts after graduation. Like Eisenhower he stated the unignorable.

We know and have known since 2001 that America's "war on terror" as well as its vain occupation of Afghanistan and its illegal invasion of Iraq with all its predictable recent implosions have usurped dollars that would and should have gone to the states. As the states tried to do what the federal government had once helped them to do, they had to work with less and less. Chancellor Nordenberg concluded that reduced federal aid to the states for higher education has already created an "innovation deficit that threatens America's leadership."

Chancellor Nordenberg is correct. Regardless, little can be done to correct this problem as long as the illegal "endless war" policies of the Bush, Cheney and Rumsfeld cabal remain in effect. Although Barack Obama was nominated and elected because of his opposition to the war, he upped the ante by sending 30,000 more troops to Afghanistan after he was elected. Many who supported him (and I was one) expected more from a Nobel Peace Awardee, but he then legalized many of the same war policies he opposed as a candidate and has added a few of his own. The "trained seals" (former Senator Abourezk's phrase) in Congress have simply gone along while silly patrioteers like Mitch McConnell and Lindsay Graham and armchair neo-con warriors, like multi-deferred Dick Cheney.

What are the consequences? The costs of the war (regardless of Secretary of Defense Hagel's projected cuts) range from $432,000,000 to $720,000,000 per day. Per day! Even the lesser figure computes to $5,000 per second. Multiply $432,000,000 by six days, and you approximate Pitt's entire operating budget for an entire year, including the medical school. Multiply it by our nearly 4000 days in Iraq, and you realize the price of folly.

The consequences for students are dire. Despite the availability of loans from the federal student loan program, the demand for aid can be expected to exceed supply. Other loan sources must be found. A friend of mine, who is an official at Notre Dame, devotes most of his time to raising money for student loans. Regardless, he told me that the average student debt upon graduation is approximately $20,000. Included in that "average" are debts of less than $20,000 while there are others over $100,000. (Nationally the median for every student debtor is $29,400 with their combined debts estimated above one trillion. Many students face 26 years of payments to clear their debts—a lifetime.) The social penalties for graduates are no less dire. A debt-carrying student might have to postpone marrying, purchasing a home or even taking a vacation.

What about the effect on colleges and universities? Some of the less reputable or on-line types try to inveigle gullible students with slick advertising that guarantees "success," as if success and not significance is the goal of higher education. The student is perceived only as a customer or a wannabe. A likely alternative for some students is to accede to the same kind of hyper advertising from the military and enlist with the hope, if they survive, of relying on G. I. Bill benefits. Meanwhile the military-industrial complex may involve them in random wars wherever the arms industries can be profitably engaged, which ignores constitutional government restraints and exploits the patriotic volunteerism of men and women in uniform.

Then there is the actual cost of tuition and board, which tops out at $50,000 to $60,000 or more per year at topnotch institutions. Unless some students receive financial aid, this translates into education only for the children of the wealthy. Meanwhile, university costs continue to climb. Many university administrators, unless they are genuine educators, reduce leadership to being bottom-liners, treating the university as a business. They cut courses in the liberal arts and humanities, which are the very core of learning, in favor of computer-driven disciplines, confusing skill with knowledge and forgetting that mere facility and the capability of making wise judgments are not synonymous. Then they exploit adjunct teachers, who teach not as a sideline but because they love and need to do it while hoping that full-time tenured positions might open up for them. Meanwhile they work for Walmart wages without benefits while still regarding teaching as their calling. The administrati who brag of large budget surpluses derived from exploiting adjuncts have the mentality of plantation owners in the Confederate South before the Civil War.

Chancellor Nordenberg has rendered a great service to academia and the general public by focusing on the price we are paying and will continue to pay unless we reject military adventurism as the illegal backdoor to the naked profiteering that it is. Considering the damage that such disregard has already done to the country and to our reputation in the eyes of much of the world, any rejections or reforms, if they come at all, will take years to make a difference. After all, we have given a complete pass to the previous administration, and its spokesmen remain at large. We have opted for amnesia instead of history, which means ignoring the hundreds of billions already squandered for a decade of war while shamelessly ignoring the human costs: 6,781 American lives lost, more than 32,000 with trauma requiring hospitalization, 320,000 with brain injuries, 1,892 officially identified by the government as suicides (exclusive of officially uncounted suicides caused by drugs as well as accidents resulting from drunk driving.) The *New York Times* has revealed that a veteran's suicide actually occurs every 80 minutes for a total of 18 suicides every day or 6,000 a year while the Veterans of Foreign Wars, in a television spot featured over Memorial Day recently, estimated one veteran's suicide every 64 minutes. Then there are Iraqi civilian deaths estimated at 1,455,590 with more than 2,000,000 Iraqis displaced. I did not invent these figures. They are in the public domain and readily accessible. We have chosen to ignore them. And if we continue to go on ignoring figures like these, we can ignore anything.

2016

30

FRAUD AND CONSEQUENCES

WHEN DOES ANNOYANCE with Bush administration policies harden into dissent? For many this seems to have happened between 2000 and 2006 when the illegal and unethical became impossible to ignore. I suspect it began in late 1999 and 2000 when the vote-by-vote recount in Florida by conscientious citizens was halted in mid-count by James Baker, Katherine Harris, Jeb Bush and others and passed on to the Supreme Court. The result was a 5 to 4 vote for George W. Bush. In effect, a selection, not an election. (The same selectivity may have occurred in 2004. Congressman John Conyers of Michigan investigated the vote results in certain disputed districts in Ohio and found irregularities that might well have changed the outcome, but no Senator but Russell Feingold would endorse his requests for a public hearing.)

Following the catastrophe of September 11, 2001 the American people were regularly made fearful by frequent terror alerts initiated by Attorney General John Ashcroft, a former Missouri Senator as well as a composer and singer of evangelical hymns. He fostered the Patriot Act, which some now see as an attempt to sidestep the Constitution. This was in the shadow of a Congressional vote (despite dissenters) that gave the President the right to wage war whenever he saw fit. To date this right has not been repealed. Despite insistence from the White House that we are at war, the war now being fought has really never been declared beyond the President's say-so.

When it became evident that Afghanistan was but a prelude to a war in Iraq (for which no *casus belli* was apparent), an unrelenting campaign to debunk and impugn the patriotism of dissenters was unleashed by the White House and the Department of Justice. Such dissenters included senators, representatives, Army and Marine generals and the majority of our allies in Europe and elsewhere. Mr. Bush's supporters were Blair of Great Britain, Berlusconi of Italy, Azner Lopez of Spain and a tossed salad of others who have since rapidly become a coalition of the less than willing. In every instance it was quite conspicuous that the populations of these countries were overwhelmingly opposed to the pro-war stances of their leaders. Regardless, the "scare" warnings from Washington became more strident. The President and Vice President, whose offices seemed to have been united by Cheney's Chief of Staff Richard Addington, ascribed everything short of treason to their opponents. Tony Blair warned that we were forty-five minutes from Armageddon, and Bush's Press Secretary Ari Fleischer at a formal news conference threatened, "People better watch what they say." This was the seed of the mentality that would eventually spawn illicit policies of arrest and detention without warrant, cover-ups of the abuse of prisoners in custody, profiling of possible suspects based on ethnicity, wire-tapping, home and computer and library searches and so on. And recently, as reported in the NEW YORK TIMES, the Department of Homeland Security is funding universities to develop "sentiment analysis hardware" to pinpoint negative opinions of the administration in letters-to-the-editor and op. ed. pieces in newspapers and magazines.

Then came the Iraq War that neo-cons like Perle, Feith, Kristol, Cheney and Rumsfeld had lobbied an all-too-willing administration into launching. They successfully denigrated Hans Blix's report that he had found no evidence of WMD in 500 Iraq locales and needed only twelve more weeks to complete his investigation. The war could not be stopped, and it was only a few months later that Bush landed on the deck of the aircraft carrier near San Diego that bannered "Mission Accomplished." Shortly after that he made a surprise visit to the troops in Iraq and was photographed bearing a *papier mache* turkey into a military dining hall.

Ahead lay the insurgency, the photographs of torture in Abu Ghraib, the deadheading transfer of captives to Guantanamo, the legal legerdemain of the new Attorney General Alberto Gonzalez, who pronounced the Geneva Conventions "quaint," in tandem with a White House attorney named John Yoo who created a rationale for "extracting" information from enemy combatants. Journalists Charles Krauthammer, William Kristol and Sean Hannity formed a chorus of support while Rush Limbaugh likened the Abu Ghraib tortures (some of which had resulted in death) to college hazing.

It seemed ironic that the impetus for the Iraq War came from the oft-deferred Dick Cheney, Paul Wolfowitz, Douglas Feith, Richard Perle, Elliot Abrams and others, none of whom, though eligible, had soldiered in the Vietnam War though they ardently supported it to the man. And the same was true of the President, whose murky time in the Air National Guard—except for the curious leave he was granted to help with the Blount campaign in Alabama—was spent defending Texas from Oklahoma. The price tag to date for the hauteur of those stalwarts was 2785 soldiers and Marines killed in action to date (an average minimum of two and a maximum of four killed each day), 20,000 wounded of which one third have suffered incapacitating wounds, the rise in suicide and post-traumatic stress rates among veterans, the ongoing cost of $10,000,000 an hour ($10,000,000 an hour!) to keep the war going and, of course, the collateral or intended deaths of civilians. The White House has disputed the deathcount of 600,000 Iraqis as calculated by independent researchers at Johns Hopkins University, but who can deal merely in arithmetic when even one death, American or otherwise, in an unjust and indefensible war of choice is one death too many?

Add to the above the errors of cronies who turned the calamity of Hurricane Katrina into a tragedy of the first order, the indictments of such allies of Mr. Bush as Kenneth Ley, Tom DeLay, Jack Abramoff, Bob Ney and Buck Cunningham, the spectacle during the recent Lebanese War when the United States balked at a cease fire while every other nation in the world with the exception of Great Britain and Israel demanded it, and Mr. Bush's silence when, as determined by

Human Rights Watch, 400,000 to 1,000,000 cluster bombs (all of which were produced by American munitions factories) were dropped in southern Lebanon on civilian targets two days before the war ended.

A burgeoning majority of voters in both parties are now joining those who have dissented from the Bush agenda from its dubious beginnings. Even previous Bush supporters are now recognizing the difference between loyalty and loyalism. Since the Bush administration itself is not subject to recall in the mid-term elections, the only weapon available for dissenters is to oust those who have backed the Bush agenda. Based on undeniable facts, it seems quite sensible that voters should ask any senatorial or congressional candidates if their support of Bush means supporting his record and then vote accordingly. If democracy means anything at all, it surely guarantees our freedom to do just that.

2006

31

BIG NUMBERS, SMALL PRINT, SMOOTH TALK, BAD RESULTS

IF PROOF BY STATISTICS and history is offensive or not persuasive to you, you should stop reading now. But if you take numerical and historic data seriously as a way of reaching unavoidable conclusions, then you're welcome to read on.

In terms of numbers the cost of one Stealth bomber is $1,157,000,000. Repeat: one billion one hundred and fifty-seven million. One plane. By way of comparison the total current annual budget for the National Endowment for the Arts is $155,000,000. The cost of a single Stealth bomber is approximately eight times that number, which means that the current total of dollars allocated for the arts throughout the country would probably be able to offset the cost of the landing gear or part of the wing of one Stealth bomber.

The federal outlay for what is termed defense (the military services plus their attendant aircraft, ships, tanks, vehicles etc.) constitutes almost a fourth of the 3.107 trillion national budget. The yearly outlay for the arts is less than one percent— .005%;

the cost per taxpayer is something close to thirty-five cents (.35) a year. (In Canada and Sweden, both with smaller population than ours, the outlay for the arts is 10%.) For further documentation of money allocated and spent for "defense," consider the following, The cost of the ongoing war in Iraq (long since proved and judged illegal, misguided and unnecessary by everyone except its initiators and those profiting from it) has been calculated at $5,000 per second. This translates into $300,000 per minute, which when multiplied by the number of minutes in an hour totals $18,000,000. Keep multiplying, and you find that the war costs $412,000,000 a day. This eventually leads you to the neighborhood of $150,000,000,000 a year. These ongoing war costs are extraordinary as well as indefensible except to say that they are meant to protect our troops in combat situations in which they should never have been involved. But multiply the aforementioned annual cost of the war by the number of years we have been in Iraq (more than seven), and you begin to see that the cost contributes mightily to the deficit, which in turn shrinks the economy, which in turn impacts the private and corporate foundations that no longer are able to support the arts as they would like. The result is that one arts organization after another disappears. This is where we find ourselves at the moment.

And look at the tawdry and jejune group of "warriors" and their stewards and lawyers who have led us to this impasse—the former President and Vice-President, the draft-evading neo-cons like Elliott Abrams and the rest. It remains inexplicable why President Obama, who is steeped in law, does not vigorously "go where the evidence leads." The statute of limitations has not expired. If justice delayed is justice denied, then injustice ignored is injustice absolved. Forget magnanimity. Vice-President Cheney publicly continues to defend the illegal practice of torture after one professional interrogator after another has testified to its immorality as well as its unreliability. And lawyers have stressed that testimony gained through torture is inadmissible in court. But Cheney goes on unchecked, and Simon & Schuster has given him a six-figure advance to continue his crusade in print. And this is the same man who ducked service four times in a Vietnam War in which he deeply believed, saying, "I had other priorities." This creed almost rhymes with that of another "true believer." It was Newt Gingrich who used as his excuse, "I thought I could serve my country better in the future." How's that for statesmanship?

All this profligacy and cowardice and hypocrisy is a matter of dishonorable record. But what does it say about us as a people? Shall we continue to suffer the consequences of all this lethal folly while ignoring or strangling those human energies that give us art, drama, literature, dance, music and poetry? These are the forms of expression that should first and foremost become us as a country and of which they are the deserved and deserving crown. What else but the arts confirm our right to feel what we feel? What else but the arts are capable of showing us who we really are? War, even when it is regrettably necessary, has as its legacy suffering, death and waste. To bring the point home, imagine the difference between war and peace as the difference between a fist and a hand. A fist is fit for punching, nothing more. A hand can, among other things, write, paint, sculpt, create music from instruments and, in doing so, inspire and heal. Of the two uses of the hand, which performs the more beneficial human act?

In the meanwhile what has become of us as a previously identified open society? Air travel has the same disconcerting flavor that one tastes when one makes an annual visit to a dentist. One hopes for a clean bill but is often confronted with the need for subsequent visits to attend to this and that. The job of screeners at our airports is the same—to root about for anything suspicious. Of course, it is small consolation when check-ups by government agents reveal that these same agents were able to board aircraft with lethal weapons on their persons or in their hand luggage that went through security undetected. The same often holds true for checkpoints at government buildings and at various buildings in the private sector. Convincing arguments have been and can be made for the necessity of pre-emptive measures (and I do not take them for granted), but the effect of these on our social lives is to make them more cramped, sour and overcast with the fog of suspicion. Moreover, it has made Security Incorporated a big and highly profitable business.

Little by little we have developed a Maginot mentality. For months before the invasion of France by Nazi Germany, the French believed that they would be protected by a line of protective trenches and forts on their eastern front. They became imprisoned and mesmerized by a sense of security that the Maginot Line offered them. In many ways we resemble the French—not in terms of dealing with an imminent threat but in the belief that our various security measures will insulate us from danger.

What about our way of life as we live and move and breathe in this cocoon of presumed security? Are we just going through the motions of normal civilian life? The televised news programs are just a breath away, if that, from packaged entertainment interspersed with sales pitches. What passes for patriotism is an affront to patriotism—lapel pins, bumper stickers, flags snapping from car antennae, bicep or buttocks tattoos, souped-up versions of the national anthem at sports events and the tag-line of "God bless America" at the conclusion of speeches whose shallowness insults both God and America. The militarization of our daily vocabulary has long been noted since the end of World War II. We are prone to "attack problems." We declare "War on Poverty." One wonders if we would be just as willing to declare "War on War." In the name of patriotism and security the level of public discourse becomes more adulterated by the day. One public official even went to the extreme of stating that French Fries should be re-christened Freedom Fries because the French had the temerity of not siding with us before and during the illegal and lethal invasion of Iraq. But this was merely the inevitable consequence of a presidential pronouncement that labeled all who were not "with us" as being "against us."

American culture in the past has shown that it is simply better than this. Civility in discourse, disturbingly absent from much of what passes for public discussion and debate of late, was once the identifying norm for what debate should be. Humor now has been sharpened into satire by and large. The happy humor of clowns finds a limited audience, proving that we have somehow lost our capacity for mirth. Newspaper journalism is not now what it once was, not only because there are fewer and fewer newspapers, but because personal animus has replaced the more reliable pursuit of facts that should ultimately be left to speak for themselves.

So here we are as we near the end of the first decade of the new century— penny-pinching Philistines where the arts are concerned, procrastinators when it comes to indicting and prosecuting known malefactors who brag publicly about their malfeasance, more ingoing than outgoing in our social outlook and civic concerns, unable or unwilling to challenge the smug morality of the ostentatiously religious and capable of putting in office peevish or undertalented individuals who invariably bring the country to its knees. In retrospect we cannot forget that Richard Nixon carried every state but Massachusetts in 1972 and that George W. Bush, though "elected" in 2000 by Judge Scalia and four associates, was, to the utter dismay of our closest allies in Europe and Latin America, re-elected in 2004. In the face of all this open mendacity and skullduggery, we have waxed indignant. We have elected a new president in the hope that conditions as we have known them will be reversed or at least identified for all to see as the cause of our indignation. But if this does not happen, will we be content to be momentarily indignant again and leave it go at that? One of the things that has been disturbingly evident since 2000 is that indignation in the face of arrogance has often been the loser. Arrogance has proceeded on its merry way. And when that happened, we retreated from indignation and even rage into indifference. And that is our problem to solve. Will we embrace the spirit of the original American Revolution and summarily demand that we live by our constitutional ideals? Or will we make an initial attempt and then, either through impatience or weakness in the face of opposition, lapse into indifference again?

2009

32

HOW MUCH IS ENOUGH?

ALBERT CAMUS WROTE that life is learning to live with one's wounds. That applies to nations as well as persons. From the latter part of the last century until now our nation has had a lot of wounds to live with, and we have survived to talk about it. We have survived an Asian war in which Lyndon Johnson changed the mission of our military from advisors to combatants on the basis of a naval incident that never happened in the Gulf of Tonkin. We have survived Richard Nixon's peevish criminality as well as his and Spiro Agnew's attempts to disembowel the press—a tactic honed to a high art lately by Karl Rove and others. We have survived the tacit okay that Alexander Haig gave to Sharon's invasion of Lebanon with the resultant loss of 14,000 lives of the inhabitants, 1,000 Israeli dead, 242 U. S. Marines blown up in a single incident and 500,000 made homeless. We have survived the machinations of one Ollie North, who bypassed Congress to funnel aid to the Contras and got away with it. We have survived the deft maneuvers of Katherine Harris, James Baker, Jeb Bush and others to swing the election of 2000 to the Supreme Court and, predictably from there, to George W. Bush. Then, under the mantra of revenge for September 11, 2001 came the illegal occupation of Iraq. Now we are condoning the invasion and demolition of Lebanon while being correctly identified by world opinion as complicit in Israeli policies. These include acts of assassination and collective punishment of Lebanese civilians, both of which are war crimes under Geneva and Nuremberg Tribunals. These inevitably provoke reprisals, and innocents on both sides die. Also, by blocking a cease-fire and by re-supplying weaponry to Israel on an expedited basis, we are spurning the Arms Export Control Act which states that "no defense article…shall be sold or leased…unless its provision will strengthen the security of the United States and promote world peace," adding that weapons sold to a friendly country may be used solely "for internal security…or maintaining or restoring international peace and security."

The question that begs to be answered as a result of all these debacles is not *why* we have survived, but *what* we have survived *to be*. Is our present government more deeply committed to constitutional principles than it was fifty years ago? Anyone who answers yes has to square his answer with recent policies allowing institutionalized torture, imprisonment without charge or trial, surveillance without warrant, abrogation of certain privacy rights, carefully orchestrated attacks on freedom of the press and freedom of information, the subordination of American foreign policy to the dictates of another country, and finally the option of the President to commit our country to a war of choice. Is our standing in the world commensurate with the respect our country commanded after World War II? Based upon recent surveys the answer is no. Is the American electorate convinced that information from government sources is to be trusted? If one uses the percentages of the major polls, the only conclusion that can be drawn is that the majority (and it is a growing majority) of voters have serious doubts about the government's view of the world compared to what they (the voters) themselves believe is the case. Those who have made these disagreements public were and occasionally still are considered unpatriotic, but that canard is rapidly losing its punch. After all, if the official positions being challenged are recognized examples of the bad judgment of the "decider" or deciders, then love of country has no place in such a debate if the dissenter or dissenters have a reasonable basis for rebuttal. Consider George W. Bush's response to Jacques Chirac when the French President told him what could happen in Iraq. Chirac had been an officer in Algeria four decades earlier and knew from first-hand experience what neo-colonial powers could expect from populations that had had their fill of invasion and occupation. "I cannot disagree with you more, Jacques," Bush is reported to have said, "Iraqis love us." For his frankness and for France's subsequent U.N. refusal to endorse the invasion, Chirac and the French were reviled. French wine was declared undrinkable and unimportable by Bill O'Reilly. French fries were re-named, and France itself in the lingo of Donald Rumsfeld was identified as a part of "old Europe." But where in all these sophomoric efforts to degrade France and its culture was there one word about historical precedent for Chirac's warning? Didn't these detractors know that no population in the history of the world has ever acquiesced (even under force or in the face of genocide) to subjugation by an outsider? Theodore Roosevelt for one would have justified all such dissent by foreign or responsible domestic sources to Bush's totalitarianism as a duty: "Patriotism means to stand by the country. It is patriotic to support (the President) insofar as he efficiently serves the country. It us unpatriotic not to oppose him to the exact extent that by inefficiency or otherwise he fails in his duty to stand by the country."

History is a harsh critic. It places little if any value on "gut instincts" or the knowledge to be gained by looking "someone in the eye." No man with any historical sense would locate the font of knowledge in the intestines, and any fool knows that the eye is as capable of deception or guile as the mouth. In the absence of genuine debate (even with elections on the horizon) the voters are left holding the bag. They will continue to pay, they will send sons, daughters, fathers and mothers on historically flawed missions (wasn't it Thomas Paine who wrote that these are invariably identified as the "noblest of causes"?), they will suffer and they will wait for some kind of deliverance. In the meanwhile they will live with their wounds, learning the hard way that bad judgments are rarely admitted by those who made them. The bitter wisdom that comes with this is that the perpetrators continue undeterred. On the very day when five soldiers were killed in Iraq (the daily deathcount is relentless) President Bush was indulging a Japanese premier's infatuation with Elvis Presley by squiring him to Graceland. The irony was surely not lost on the next of kin. But what could they or anyone do? Between a false triumphalism on the one hand and defeatism or despair on the other, living with one's wounds while dissenting from those whose policies inflicted them is about as dignified an alternative as there is at the moment. Not much, but something.

2006

33

A WAR FOR ALL SEASONS

THE LAST BOOK that Arthur Miller published before his death dealt with politics as theater. Focusing on the last thirty years, he concluded that politics was becoming more theatrical—more and more packaged and staged. As a man of the theater, he had a point. What with television, scripted speeches, make-up and so-called presidential debates that resemble tightly moderated quiz shows, it seems that political theater is here to stay. Candidates book themselves on Oprah and Letterman and pretend they are more than entertainment while issues of life and death are not openly faced and discussed. And the news programs with rare exceptions have followed a similar scenario—shouting matches on cable counterpointed by network news that is orchestrated for ratings by opening with something grave and concluding with a snippet that is inspiring, heartwarming or humorous. Mankind cannot stand too much reality, said T. S. Eliot, and politics as theater has provided us with an excuse for hiding from reality indefinitely.

It was Churchill who said that "facts are better than dreams." If he were alive today, he would probably say that facts are decidedly worse than dreams. The harsh facts of this decade have long since made a mockery of Bush's "Mission Accomplished." If you accept the vision of the neo-conservatives, who are adept at prosecuting wars with other people's sons and daughters and with other people's money, it seems that we are in a struggle that will last forever. People like Cheney, Rumsfeld, Perle, Boykin and the rest are on record as saying so. They are also on record as sanctioning preventive war, torture, wiretapping without warrant, assassinations and the entire chromatic scale of methods designed to defend what they have dubbed the homeland. The consequences for our constitutional democracy are ominous. President Obama, whose election I welcomed, has to date reversed too few of these mandates. His decision to look ahead rather than back is hardly an answer. History did not begin with his inauguration. Had he chosen to investigate or at least question his predecessors, much could have been learned from those who placed us in this quandary, but the miscreants who created our dilemmas have thus far been given a free pass.

Take the Iraq War as evidence. It is now universally conceded that this war of choice was illegal by our own and international standards. That it was done to create democracy in Iraq was mocked when the man chosen in the purple-fingered election was re-placed by a man of our preference. That the country is "pacified" is contradicted by daily bombings. The human cost includes more than two million Iraqis who have left the country, more than 150,000 who have been killed, thousands who have been maimed and the culture ravaged. For us it has meant 4,300 killed and counting, tens of thousands wounded physically and psychologically, hundreds driven to suicide and internationalizing the National Guard. The Marine Corps and the Army have been strained to the breaking point and forced to rely on multiple deployments or to give AWOL service men a choice of serving prison sentences or opting for additional tours in Iraq in order to meet "volunteer" quotas. Then there is the ongoing cost calculated at $5,000 a second or $300,000 a minute or $18,000,000 an hour or $432,000,000 a day or $147,930,000,000 a year. Then multiply the latter number by seven, which is how many years we have occupied Iraq, and you reach figures that baffle comprehension. To make these figures real, consider that the expenditure of a single year of the war would underwrite the cost of running one American university of 10,000 boarding students for 150 years without anyone's having to raise a single endowment dime. Add to the war cost the funding used to re-construct a country (which we "deconstructed") by American companies in no-bid contracts, and you have a perfect example of how the military-industrial complex works, which Naomi Klein has correctly identified as "disaster capitalism." Then add the budgets for Blackwater and other private contractors, who equal in numbers the military personnel already there, and… But why go on? Cheney the draft-evader and infallible millionaire has said that deficits don't matter, and no one bats an eye. But what about soldiers' lives? Do they matter?

Now comes Afghanistan. Kept on the back burner for more than five years, it is now in the forefront. The President has called it "a war of necessity," but he has not defined "necessity." The outspoken General McChrystal has said he can win the war in a decade, and, if he prevails, we can assume that the 40,000 replacements he has requested will be followed by another request, a la General Westmoreland in a previous war, for 40,000 more and so on. The Pentagon, according to historian William R. Polk, is already projecting a war of fifty years in their planning at a cost of trillions. McChrystal's boss, General Petraeus, is on record as calling the war unwinnable, which makes for a curious imbalance, to say the least. But there is unanimous agreement among all that the Karzai government is corrupt. Unless my logic is faulty this leaves us in an open-ended unwinnable war to maintain a corrupt government at a cost that will further impoverish our already hard-pressed citizenry while simultaneously costing the lives of American service man and women and uncountable Afghans. Imagine Marines and Army units going into battle with that mantra as their motivation!

Arthur Miller's aforementioned book on politics as theater (ON POLITICS AND THE ART OF ACTING) was published before the catastrophic events of September 11, 2001. But he appeared in Pittsburgh in October of that year to give an address in the Heinz Lecture Series. Using that book as the theme of his speech, he seemed to have a sense of foreboding about of what he feared might happen, namely, that the theatrical manipulators in the White House at that time would somehow spin the anxiety that was rampant in the country to their advantage. Miller was a man who possessed a tragic sense, and he seemed to know that the worst can happen after we think that the worst is behind us. He implied that a genuine sense of the tragic seemed to be absent in the Bush White House. And the consequences of that absence are playing out now, albeit in a different administration. The figures and statements I have cited in this short essay did not originate with me. They are all a matter of public record and are readily verifiable. One can only hope that the current incumbent is not only intelligent enough (he is) but decisive enough (is he?) to be aware of them and to reverse what could repeat itself as farce, to borrow an old maxim, or, as much as we dread it, further tragedy.

2009

34

THE ONGOING DUPING OF AMERICA

"All governments lie," wrote the pundit and loner I. F. Stone. Some may lie more convincingly than others, but lie they all do. And when the lies have tragic consequences, they rationalize (lie) to justify or gloss over the original lies. Of course, stating this is nothing new. We have heard and said it thousands of times. But have we listened carefully to what we have said? Or have we been so deflated by mendacity in government that we have "retreated" into passivity and pessimism when our response should have begotten more activism in us, not less.

Why, for example, do we still believe or refuse to face the lies about Vietnam? We now know definitively that John Kennedy had ordered the removal of American troops by 1965. This is not a footnote to the casual but truthful aside that Oliver Stone stated in conjunction with the first public showing of his Vietnam film PLATOON. This is thoroughly documented by Gordon M. Goldstein in LESSONS IN DISASTER: MCGEORGE BUNDY AND THE PATH TO WAR IN VIETNAM.

Goldstein, by the way, was Bundy's co-editor of his collected letters when the latter was preparing them for publication, so his knowledge is the knowledge of an insider. But after the murder of Kennedy, it was Lyndon Johnson who rammed through Congress the Tonkin Gulf Resolution (opposed only by two senators then—Wayne Morse and Ernest Gruening—, both of whom were defeated for re-election). It has been shown since that there was no naval incident in the Gulf of Tonkin and that the resolution was a trumped-up justification for Johnson to raise the stakes in Vietnam ("I don't want Ho Chi Minh to spit in my eye, and I don't want to spit in his eye.") The rest is unforgettable history we deliberately forget.

Richard Nixon was elected in 1968 by promising to end the war. Instead he widened it illegally into Cambodia. The result was that more American servicemen died after 1968 than before. However, the duping of the public worked, and Nixon—we must remember—did what no presidential candidate did before or has done since. He won every state but Massachusetts in 1972. That to me is a more significant symptom of the malady of the electorate than the fact that Nixon was forced from office only a few years later. But Vietnam demonstrated ultimately that the domino theory was a guess based on an illusion. The bare, unaccepted truth (and it continues to be and will always be true) was and is that no occupiers and invaders from abroad can defeat an indigenous and antagonistic people. Why? Because the invaders can and will eventually leave, but the native population has no other place to go. However long their suffering and however brutal their suppression, the indigenous will eventually prevail. That is why the bravado of people like Curtis LeMay, who advocated bombing North Vietnam back to the Stone Age, is now seen for what it was—the bravado of a hubristic general who was on the side of death, not history.

The duping of America continued in the first decade of the twenty-first century. The pretexts for the Iraq War have long since been exposed for the lies they were as stated by the then President, Vice-President, Secretary of State and the compliant Tony Blair. But, as in the late sixties and seventies, the duping worked again. Bush was inexplicably re-elected in 2004 because, under the tutelage of Rove, he ran as a war president whose defeat in the election, as the story went, would undermine the war effort against eternal evil and render meaningless the lives that had already been sacrificed.

One of the latent ironies that became apparent during the run-up to the war was that the duping did not seem to convince the leaders of almost all of the organized religions. Methodist, Presbyterian, Episcopalian, Catholic and rabbinical denominations openly claimed that the war in the offing in Iraq could not be justified. The then pope, John Paul II, unambiguously stated his opposition and maintained it (as does his successor) through the remainder of his papacy. Nonetheless all the denominations that opposed the war-to-be were conspicuously silent after the war began and remain so. This included the National Council of Catholic Bishops, which curiously was not persuaded by John Paul II's opposition. This is either an example of the effects of delayed duping or an instance where the bishops were in possession of information or moral dispensations denied the rest of mankind.

Now despite Bush's departure from the national scene, the duping has carried over inasmuch as many of the previous administration's policies, long since proved both immoral, illegal and unproductive, are still in effect, i.e., use of torture on prisoners by us or our proxies in black sites, wire-tapping, arrest and possible deportation on the basis of suspicion alone and so on. The neo-conservatives who were responsible for this are still audible from their cockpits at universities, think tanks, federal institutions and the administration itself.

The current duping now extends to Afghanistan. Despite General McChrystal's early assurance that he could pacify a country that has not been conquered, as William Pfaff reminds us in his recent THE IRONY OF MANIFEST DESTINY, since Alexander the Great, the ongoing human tolls keep rising. (THE NEW YORK TIMES block-prints the names of the American dead daily.) Few state unequivocally that Americans are dying for a government there that is demonstrably corrupt. Even the now fired McChrystal, who should have been fired earlier when he aired his views of the war to the press even before meeting with the President, had recently scaled back his early optimism. His endgame could most charitably be described as endless, and his successor has indicated that there would be no basic change in policy.

Again, regardless of the contradicting facts, the duping goes on to reveal nothing but an outlook infected by triumphalism and a wished-for reality. And then there is the blind fidelity of our country to allies and clients whose actions fly in the face of what we ought to stand for. Israel is the current case in point. Overlooking (if that is possible) the recent commandeering of a ship in international waters, Israel continues to imprison or otherwise occupy and dominate a Palestinian population longer (50 years and counting) in the West Bank and Gaza than any comparable historical parallel with no end in sight. In the name of security, Israel guards (and defines) borders and has complete control of entry or egress by land, sea or sky—the very definition of imprisonment. The neo-cons support this, and compliant congressmen and American taxpayers say or do little to change the policy. Indeed, we are seen as complicit despite the fact that a Jewish intelligentsia in Israel, America and elsewhere—David Grossman, Tony Judt, Uri Avinery, Sara Roy, Noam Chomsky, Richard Falk, Roger Cohen, Norman Finklestein, Rabbi Marc Ellis, George Soros, Rabbis for Peace, Howard Zinn and the late Tanya Rinehart—-have courageously expressed their opposition. They also opposed the onslaught on Lebanon in 2006, which our government could have stopped but permitted to go on until the deaths, casualties and displacements in the country exceeded tens of thousands and was justly identified as collective punishment. A recent facsimile occurred in the Israeli invasion and ravaging of Gaza, which we could have stopped but did not. Under what law, moral or otherwise, can such wars be justified, and to what purpose?

Of course, the duping will go on, regardless of words like these or anything similar. But I recently saw a scene in a television documentary that showed the reality of war and loss for what they were whether in Iraq, Afghanistan or the Middle East. The mother of a captain killed by snipers in Iraq was showing the interviewer a letter she received from her son that was postmarked on the day he died. She said she read it often.

But each time she closed the envelope, she slowly licked it shut so that her tongue could taste her son in the last thing he ever touched. If that's not enough to shame the dupers into recanting their duplicity or keeping it to themselves so as not to cause further trouble for the good of our country, nothing can.

2010

35

NO RHYME OR REASON FOR HYPHENS

MAN IS A BORN NAME-GIVER. It started with Adam, and it continues to this day. We live under the compulsion to name things so that we can know them. This is our mission, and, provided we name things according to their natures, it is a worthy and daily necessity in our lives. It constitutes what we all eventually recognize as knowledge.

A danger arises when we are inclined to name things, not according to their natures, but in accordance with categories or blocs or traditions in which we think they belong. I believe, as I hope to demonstrate, that this is not only false knowledge but debilitating to our way of understanding the world. For writers it is something to be avoided at all costs. John Henry Newman has said that literature is the autobiography of man. I would insist that literature is the autobiography of men and women in all their individuality but with universal implications. Anyone who reads poetry or fiction knows exactly what that means. But in our day-to-day lives there are numerous social forces that constantly strive to pluralize us or otherwise subsume us into categories where our individualities—our true selves—are lost. And our humanity pays the price. We are not what we are but how we are seen. To some we are simply consumers. To others we are voters. To still others we are notch-babies, and so on.

Even if we acknowledge that categories such as the few that I've mentioned do not reveal who we really are, we often perpetuate these same generalizing tendencies when we seek to identify ourselves. Take nationality as a case in point. With the exception of religion, there is probably no subject that provokes more controversy than nationality. And the controversy invariably results from how the term is defined—or ill-defined.

It is a basic political fact that the nation to which you owe your allegiance defines your nationality. If you are a *bona fide* citizen of the United States, your nationality is American. If you are a citizen of Canada, you are a Canadian. If you are from Finland, you are a Finn. As a United States citizen you are instantly identified and identifiable as such when you travel abroad. Your passport attests to it. When you fill out your visa forms, you write "American" in the space reserved for nationality.

Ironically, this practice does not carry over into civic life in the United States.

Some years ago I conducted an exercise with a group of thirty college students of mine when I asked them one by one to identify themselves by nationality. And one by one the wrong answers came: Polish, Irish, German Irish, Italian, Taiwanese, Greek and the rest. Of the thirty only one student identified himself as an American, and he was a transfer student from

Harlem. The other twenty-nine accused me candidly of throwing them off by my asking them to reveal their nationalities. They assumed, as the majority of Americans assume, that nationality and ethnicity were the same. I then referred them to the true meaning of nationality, which in our country has nothing to do with ethnic heritage, just as it has nothing to do with race, gender, age or religion, but is simply based on allegiance to the Constitution as amended.

When this concept of nationality or citizenship was first proclaimed in the eighteenth century, it was a revolutionary concept. While the people of other countries had a genetic, racial or ethnic blood base in common, the United States based citizenship on voluntary assent to the Constitutional principles of its founding. It has rightly been called an experiment in governance. And there are some who say that such an experiment can well fail because a common ethnicity is absent.

I have already indicated that many Americans have no hesitancy in identifying themselves as Americans when they are abroad, but back in the United States they invariably define themselves in terms of their ethnic heritage. It seems ironic that an American should feel more American in Europe than in Pennsylvania, for instance, but such is often the case. I do not make this point as a matter of chauvinism, which I find an obnoxious vanity, but as a matter of observable fact. In political life the fudging of citizenship and ethnicity is now part of the DNA of national elections. Voters are identified by hyphenation in blocs: Italo-Americans, Afro-Americans, Irish-Americans, Hispanic-Americans and, of course, Arab-Americans.

Politicians who target audiences in this way do not do the American experiment a favor. In fact, they contribute to the dumbing down of the electorate by appealing not to the mind but to the blood. And any serious student of history knows the mischief that can come and has come from that. Even more mischievous is acceptance of the existence of dual citizenship, which boils down to the fact that a person can be a citizen of two countries simultaneously. One wonders what would happen if, in a crisis, such a person would have to choose one or the other. This strikes me, regardless of the advantages that might be forthcoming from dual citizenship, as being as contradictory and ill-advised as bigamy.

Apart from the political implications attached to nationality, hyphenated or straight, what are the implications for a writer, particularly though not exclusively, if he is of Middle Eastern heritage? I contend that the implications would be the same for him or her as they would be for any citizen, whatever the ethnic background might be. A true writer writes from his sensibility—from what he senses or intuits as an individual human being. He cannot write out of sense of ethnicity alone, or he is writing primarily for his fellow ethnics. Richard Wright warned black writers in the middle of the last century that they would be writing only for and to one another if all their motivation to write came from racial consciousness. And he was and is right. Substitute ethnicity for race, and the same principle applies.

Consider the struggle of the Irish for independence as a case in point. Having suffered for centuries under British colonial occupation and duress, they had reason enough to write poems and songs of resistance. And they did. And many of them were and remain stirring. But in some ways they serve the same purpose that cheerleaders or rhetoricians serve. They play to the crowd, and it is for the arousal of the crowd that the written, spoken or sung words are intended. Such words resonate most viscerally on home grounds. But a poet or a poet-in-prose invariably transcends boundaries. Compare the Irish ballad about the martyr Frank Duggan, stirring as it is, with the quiet but unforgettable lines of Lionel Johnson's poem about the Gaelic language: "That speech that wakes the soul in tired faces/And wakes remembrance of great days gone by." And then you have the example of William Butler Yeats, who would have remained a poet in the Irish lyrical and romantic tradition had not the "troubles" changed him, to use his word, "utterly." Had it not been for that change, we would know him primarily as the author of "The Ballad of the Wandering Aengus" and not as the man who realized after the leaders of the revolt were executed that a "terrible beauty is born." It was then that he could write "The Second Coming" in which the implosion of any disintegrating society is prefigured in lines that are as applicable to Ireland as they would be to Poland or any country on the face of the earth, ours at this moment particularly included.

> Turning and turning in the widen gyre,
> The falcon cannot hear the falconer;
> Things fall apart; the centre cannot hold;
> Mere anarchy is loosed upon the world.
> The blood-dimmed tide is loosed, and everywhere
> The ceremony of innocence is drowned;

> The best lack all conviction, while the worst
> Are full of passionate intensity…

And what of Bertolt Brecht's prescient lines before the outbreak of World War II? Written almost seventy years ago, is their real meaning confined to the time of their composition? Is it restricted in its reference to Nazi Germany alone, or are the implications dateless and international? "The common people know that war is coming./When the leaders talk peace,/ the mobilization orders have already been signed."

Creative writers whose lineage is Middle Eastern must live up to no less a standard than that faced by Lionel Johnson, William Butler Yeats and Bertolt Brecht. In other words, their work must transcend ethnicity—even if their subject is an ethnic one. Otherwise it becomes not literature but something close to sociology.

It is not the subject but the writer's attitude and feeling for the subject that tells us whether it is poetry or not. In short, it is his sensibility that spawns the poem. Even the meaning of the word *poet* in Arabic affirms that. For the Greeks a poet (*pietis* or *pietria)* is one who makes. For the Russians a poet is he who leads. For numerous other cultures the poet is thought of as a seer, a visionary. This goes back to the Old Testament where the prophets were so regarded—not as men who could predict what would happen but as those who could truly see the present and say so. This was and is a dangerous calling. But for the Arabs the poet has always been seen as one who feels. The poetry is in the feeling.

Let me cite two poems as examples by poets of Arabic lineage that reveal what I mean. I have chosen poems by Naomi Shihab Nye and Hayan Charara to show how their visions of two different subjects suddenly and feelingly universalizes those subjects for us. They transcend lineage by subsuming it.

Naomi Shihab Nye is now widely known both in this country and abroad, and she has written poignantly of the tragedy in the Middle East, beginning with the Palestinians and now involving Iraq. I could cite several poems of hers like "Blood" and "Lunch in Nablus City Park" and others that show her sensitivity to human suffering, but I have chosen the following because it is uniquely American. And yet I venture to say that it could only have been written by someone who was touched and aroused spiritually by what it describes. The poem is called "He Said EYE-RACK."

> Relative to our plans for your country
> we will blast your tree, crush your cart,
> stun your grocery.
> Amen brothers and sisters,
> give us your sesame legs,
> your satchels, your skies.
> Freedom will feel good
> to you too. Please acknowledge
> our higher purpose. No, we did not see
> your bed of parsley. On St. Patrick's Day
> 2003 President Bush wore a blue tie. Blinking hard,
> he said, "We are not dealing with peaceful men."
> He said, "reckless aggression."
> He said, "the danger is clear."
> Your patio was not visible in his frame.
> Your comforter stuffed with wool

from a sheep you knew. He said, "We are
against the lawless men who
rule your country, not you." Tell that
to the mother, the sister, the bride,
the proud boy, the peanut seller,
the librarian careful with her shelves.
The teacher, the spinner, the sweeper,
the invisible village, the thousands of people
with laundry and bread, the ants tunneling
through the dirt.

Hayan Charara is widely known as a poet and also as the editor of INCLINED TO SPEAK, an anthology of poems by Americans of Arab extraction. I say this in keeping with my complaint about the hyphen since Arab-American is for me an oxymoron like all others that fudge ethnicity with allegiance and what follows from allegiance, i.e., an individual's cultural identity. This is one of his poems, an elegy to his mother entitled "Unfinished Business" from his book entitled THE SADNESS OF OTHERS. The sound that you hear as the poem unfolds is the sound of a heart, breaking.

My father refused to donate
her clothes to the Salvation Army.
The long-sleeved shirt
she had tossed
into the laundry basket
the morning she died
he hung in their bedroom closet,
the lingering smell of her perfume
a reminder in case he forgets.
Her shoes are still
at the bottom of the stairwell.

Her purse, everything in it,
remains undisturbed
behind the dresser,
the expired driver's license,
grade school photographs
of my sister and me,
a disposable lighter,
butterscotch drops,
and the keys to her Ford,
which he has left parked at the curb
for the last two years.

Since I am the son of parents who immigrated to Pittsburgh from Jerusalem and a small village in the south of Lebanon in the early part of the last century, I have written a sheaf of poems over the years that reflect that lineage and that orientation—some of them familial and others on related themes. I can only hope that they live up to the standard I have tried to validate in this address, namely, that they have more than an ethnic character and appeal. That will be for you to judge.

The first is an elegy to my grandfather. One of his pleasures was singing with my mother. Both of them played the lute or oud. After her death he continued the tradition but always with an undertone of sadness. This is how I remember him.

Someone should speak a word for you
who after all lived only long
enough to teach us children's songs
in Arabic remembered now

with times you strung your lute alone
and plucked it with an eagle's plume

while we sat quiet, small and calm
and heard you sing of Lebanon

until your days of roundelays
turned brief as breathing, and the vengeance
of cathedrals tolled to silence
all your love and all your minstrelsy.

I still remember the words in those songs, but I keep them to myself since my Arabic can best be described as unreliable. I can only hope that the heart of that short poem to my grandfather touches the feelings of all who have a special love for the parents of their parents.

In our era the volatile history of the Middle East almost inevitably forces itself on our attention because of our ancestry but also because the suffering of people in the Middle East is bound up with the suffering of people everywhere. If we respond to the suffering of people in Lebanon or Palestine, for example, and not to the suffering of people in similar circumstances elsewhere, we are lacking in what can only be called the milk of human kindness and the universal hunger for justice for all. Unavoidably, political considerations will try to find their way into our writing, whether it be poetry or fiction or history or the personal essay. It certainly did for Yeats, and because of that Yeats is now recognized as a great poet of the world and not simply of Ireland. And it was Leo Tolstoy who pointed out the difference between literature that was narrowly partisan and literature that recognized nothing less than the solidarity of flesh and blood. "Political literature, reflecting the transitory interests of society," wrote Tolstoy, "has its importance, yet, however necessary to the people's development, there still exists another literature that echoes the eternal preoccupations shared by all mankind, and which contains creations precious to the heart of the people, a literature accessible to the man of any class, and without which no vigorous population full of strength has ever developed."

Years ago my wife and I traveled by car (a Volkswagen) from Beirut to Jerusalem. After a border crossing in Syria we drove due south to Jericho, then up to Jerusalem. This was pre-1967 so that my concern was totally with the road and geography. Oriented toward Western culture via Europe and England, I felt a definite difference in myself by being where I was. Apart from the car and the highway, the time could have been centuries earlier. I had a totally different sense of time as we drove. This was beyond ethnicity, and years later when that trip became a poem I somehow managed to put into that poem the sense of estrangement and even mystery that I experienced as a western traveler in the Middle East.

> As I drive south to Christ and Abraham,
> the tires speed the desert road before
> me back to Syria. The clocks have stopped.
> Only the sky turns modern when a jet
> veers eastward for Bombay. Below
> its powered wings stand sheep and Bedouin.
>
> The sun blinks at me from a donkey's eye
> exactly as it blinked eight centuries
> ago on tribes of Arabs armed to purge
> the last crusader from Jerusalem.
> How many bones survive? How many skulls
> did Timurlane leave stacked in pyramids

where Bedouin fork wheat against the wind
and watch it fall. I squint for evidence.
The deadness of the sea near Jericho
unscrolls no secrets, and the sand endures
for wind alone to sift and re-arrange
and blow the smell of Briton, Frenchman, Turk

and Mongol to the sun. The time is what
it was when Sarah laughed the angel back
to God. She shepherds wait for Christ. The tribes
of Canaan graze their camels near the road
I conquer like a new crusader armed
with film and cigarettes. Nursed on the blood

of Europe's cross and Europe's rack, I search
for what was here before the world moved west.
A donkey blinks. Bedouin cane their sheep.
A child cries until his mother plumps
her breast against him, thumbs the nipple firm
and plugs the blind mouth mute as history.

That trip further immersed me in the tragedy of the Palestinians in a face-to-face way, and that has never vanished. Indeed, it is even more intense today because their situation has become even more dire. Yet it all now has a human face because of a chance encounter I had with a young shoeshine boy in the streets of Jerusalem on that trip. Some of the details have faded, but the memory is still vivid. It is in regard to this poem that I ask you to judge if it is a genuine poem or simply the "political literature" that Tolstoy considered to be, however necessary and important in its time, spiritually secondary. Here is the poem entitled “For Fawzi in Jerusalem.”

Leaving a world too old to name
and too undying to forsake,
I flew the cold, expensive sea
toward Columbus’ mistake
where life could never be the same

for me. In Jerash on the sand
I saw the colonnades of Rome
bleach in the sun like skeletons.
Behind a convalescent home,
armed soldiers guarded no man’s land

between Jordanians and Jews.
Opposing sentries frowned and spat.
Fawzi, you mocked in Arabic
this justice from Jehoshophat
before you shined my Pittsburgh shoes

for nothing. Why you never kept
the coins I offered you is still
your secret and your victory.
Saying you saw marauders kill
your father while Beershebans wept

for mercy in their holy war,
you told me how you stole to stay
alive. You must have thought I thought
your history would make me pay
a couple of piastres more

than any shine was worth—and I
was ready to—when you said, "No,
I never take. I never want
American to think I throw
myself on you. I never lie."

I watched your young but old man's stare
demand the sword to flash again
in blood and flame from Jericho
and leave the bones of these new men
of Judah bleaching in the air

like Roman stones upon the plain
of Jerash. Then you faced away.
Jerusalem, Jerusalem,
I asked myself if I could hope
for peace and not recall the pain

you spoke. But what could hoping do?
Today I live your loss in no
man's land but mine, and every time
I talk of fates, not just but so,
Fawzi, my friend, I think of you.

Since all people hate to have their homes or their countries occupied by strangers by force, they inevitably endure it until their hatred of their oppressors overcomes their fear of them—when they hate what they fear more than they fear it. Compare it with the resistance of the Irish against the British, of the Norwegians and French against the Nazis, of the Algerians against the French and so on. History provides no lack of examples, but John Steinbeck in THE MOON IS DOWN said in a single sentence what is at the core of all such efforts by those who seek to suppress others by force when he wrote: “The flies have conquered with flypaper.” I know of no poem that sides with the oppressors, but I can name many that speak for the oppressed, and the voice that I hear in those poems is the voice of freedom-loving people everywhere, and I think Tolstoy would confirm that it “echoes the eternal preoccupations common to all mankind.”

I will conclude with what came to me as I was watching the American flag on a flagpole just outside my office being lashed and slashed by high winds. The flag in utter defiance withstood the shredding wind even though it was damaged. It somehow seemed to symbolize our national condition. The images that this scene prompted lead me back to affirm what I have suggested throughout this essay, namely, that our writings as Americans will be judged as American literature or nothing at all. There is no such thing as a hyphenated literature in the United States or in any other country in the world. We will be read and judged as American writers first and foremost. If what we write, whatever the subject may be, does not transcend our geography or our lineage, then we are not only less American but less the writers we presume to be. Those who choose to see Americans in terms of hyphenated identity are in the same business as those who in political terms seek to divide and conquer. Leave hyphenation to the sociologists and the followers of family trees. Apply it to literature, and you end with books being segregated in special shelves devoted to ethnic literature. In the same spirit nationalistic poetry or fiction is an oxymoron. It must be international and timeless, or it is simply not literature. And we identify with the author not because of his genes but because of his sensibility. He must touch us through his words as a human being first, last and always. That makes what he writes subject to no other criterion than that established by Horace: "I am human, and nothing human is alien to me." (Ego homo, et nihil mihi humanum alienum est.)

Crosswinds have slashed the flag
so that that the thirteenth ribbon
dangles free or coils around
the flagpole like a stripe.
What's left
keeps fluttering in red-and-white
defiance.
Somehow the tattering
seems apropos.
The President
proclaims we'll be at war forever—
not war for peace but war
upon war, though hopefully not here.
Believers in eternal re-election
hear his pitch and pay.
In Washington
God's lawyer warns we stand
at Armageddon, and we battle
for the Lord.
Elsewhere, California's
governor believes in California's
governor, and football bowls
are named for Mastercard, Pacific
Life, Con-Agra and Tostitos.
Out west a plan to gerrymander
Colorado (Texas-style) fails,
but barely.

Asked why no flag
is studded in his coat lapel
or decorates his aerial, a veteran
responds, "I wear my flag
on my heart—I don't wear
my heart on my sleeve."
Today
for once we're spared the names
of occupying soldiers shot
or rocketed to fragments in Iraq.
Collateral damage?
Two boys,
their mother and both grandparents.
No names for them…
Just Arabs.

2009

36

FROM THE PURPOSE OF SPORT

SPORT IS DEFINED as activity done for enjoyment. In short, play. In its purest form it is found in recreation and in amateur athletics. Internationally speaking, it reaches its apogee in the Olympic Games (summer or winter) where all the participating athletes swear an oath that they will perform for the "glory of sport." The ancients Greeks, who originated the Games, added the final and most enduring honor by stating: "Nothing can take away from a man what he has done with his hands and his feet." History has proved them both prescient and correct. Think of Jesse Owens, Paavo Nurmi, Muhammad Ali when he fought under the name of Cassius Marcellus Clay, Bob Mathias, Mike Eruzione who refused to "go pro" because he wanted nothing to eclipse the American hockey team's defeat of the favored Russians in Lake Placid in 1980, Adebe Bikila the barefooted distance runner from Ethiopia who dominated the Olympics in his era, Jean Benoit, Mark Spitz and the great undefeated Cuban heavyweight Theofilo Stevenson who thought that becoming a professional heavyweight contender was a "step down."

But what happens to sport (or sports) in a society when play is professionalized—when what is done is done for money or for nothing short of ultimate domination (championships) by individuals or teams? In such cases, the "glory of sport" becomes a secondary consideration. Despite the hoopla and expressions of team loyalty and the like, the things that seem to count in recent decades are rankings, salaries, statistics and getting favorable "ink." This has become even more the case as salaries, revenues and expenses have risen astronomically. The players themselves recognize this at trade times when they shrug and say frankly, "It's a business."

Being a business, sports franchises require a strong and growing fan base. Playing for pay demands payers from today's version of everyone from bleacherites to owners of private boxes. And because the victory-addicted appetites of fans must be regularly satisfied (or they won't continue to "pay"), the owners are under constant strain to keep teams and athletes in contention—"in the hunt." In our era this has driven some athletes to the use of steroids and other drugs, performance-enhancing or not. At times this has led to their deaths (as probably was the case with Lyle Alzado and definitely with Len Bias), but it seemed to promise a way for them to keep pace or to perform when hurt, bandaged or numbed for the sake of the champagne shower at season's end. And there are other costs. It has been medically estimated that 100% of all professional football players retire from the game with permanent injuries to the knee and neck. The injuries may show up immediately upon retirement or later, as was the case with a wheelchair-bound Jim Otto. And there is the matter of head trauma, somewhat second-tiered until recently. All these are part of the price paid and occasionally admitted. No less a luminary than Joe Namath was quoted several years ago as saying, "I would give all my money and my houses and my cars if I could only put my pants on by myself."

No one disputes that professional sports are a financial boon to a select group of athletically talented men and women who do whatever it is they do remarkably well. No one disputes that professional teams contribute mightily to civic pride and deportment. I was a visiting professor in Detroit when the Tigers won the pennant, and it was conceded by one and all, including Mayor Jerome Cavanaugh, that only the pennant race kept the lid on city violence at that time. Teams also make possible the creation of ancillary spin-off enterprises—sports paraphernalia, shoe-wear, textiles. And, finally, no one denies that the national sports maw is insatiable. So professional sports are here to stay.

Leaving aside the scandals and other distractions, what about the effects of professional sports upon the country as a whole The most obvious and often annoying effect is that sports, like politics, education and too much of our public life, has been linked to entertainment. Everything from the hoopla of national conventions to bobble-heads to half-time shows and the electronic circus of the scoreboard (and even the occasional pre-game jazzed-up singing of the national anthem) play to the crowd. The warm-up to the Super Bowl lacks for nothing, and the half-time show has all the trappings of the Second

Coming. Even the announced entrance of the players and the overdone celebrations in the end zone after a score are exaggerated. I find myself remembering with both nostalgia and fondness the understated, all-in-the-line-of-work deportment of Franco Harris when he scored a touchdown, even the one that resulted from the Immaculate Reception. No high-fiving, hip-bumping, chest-thumping or other Tarzan-like gestures—no self-proclamations of greatness.

It leaves us asking when does sport become show? Or has it been irreparably reduced to show already? Of course, there are exceptions, and the exceptions are deserving of recognition since some glimmer of the "glory of sport" still survives there. I have already mentioned Franco Harris, and I could easily add the name of Lynn Swann. Then there was the recent national basketball playoff between Duke and Butler in Indianapolis. Farther back during the 1984 winter Olympic Games in Chamonix, the great skier Jean-Claude Kiely won his third gold medal. Prominent in the crowd was the President of France, Charles de Gaulle. I think it was Howard Cosell or someone equally pushy who approached Kiely and said, "Jean-Claude, this must be one the greatest moments in your life…to win your third Olympic Gold Medal in the presence of President de Gaulle!" Kiely looked down at his skies and said quietly, "In my sporting life." And there is the unique pitcher Randy "Big Unit" Johnson, who responded to a burst of overdone accolades by saying, "But it's just a game." And finally there is the deportment of a Notre Dame quarterback of yesteryear named John Huarte. When his name was announced as the winner of the Heisman Trophy in 1964, he left his seat on stage, walked to the table where his mother and father were seated, kissed his mother and father and only then returned to the microphone to thank Coach Ara Parseghian and his team mates. These are small moments, to be sure, but they show a modesty and manliness that are really at the core of the "glory of sport" as well as a mark of, for lack of a better word, class.

2010

37

THE GLORY OF SPORT

ARE WE AMERICANS SPORTS-CRAZY? Based upon casual observation, I would say we are. But why?

The answers I have found are many, and they apply equally to all major sports: baseball, football, basketball, hockey, track and the Olympics. One distinguished basketball coach told me that Americans love sports because this gives them an emotional outlet, an alternative to their usual occupations, a way of indulging their competitive instincts, as it were, by proxy. Others say that watching gifted athletes performing under pressure enlivens a spirit of civic or national camaraderie. Still others claim that we have an insatiable desire for victory because frankly we are a people who can't not win, unlike, for example, the French who seem to appreciate style of play as much as the outcome.

There is some merit in all of these reasons, but I think there is a deeper reason. It's rarely mentioned or acknowledged, but it's the one that makes all the others possible. It springs, I believe, from one of our deepest needs—a hunger to see justice done. In sports such justice translates as fairness. In amateur or professional sports we must be assured in advance and in practice that the "rules of the game" will be strictly enforced. If not, the spirit of sport becomes a sham.

In public life we all hope to see merit acknowledged and rewarded with wrongdoing recognized for what it is. But our hopes are often mocked, dashed or trivialized in matters of commerce, government or religion. In our corporately top-heavy society it's not unusual, for example, to learn of CEO's and other high-level functionaries charged with profiteering and such but getting off Scot-free while their underlings bear the blame. In 2000 the Supreme Court gifted George W. Bush with the presidency, which Justice Breyer called unforgivable in his dissent, and at the end of the decade made corporate largesse to candidates both unlimited and legal. So much for the democratic process… After nine years of wars that have been universally recognized as illegal and immoral, the architects of these wars (Bush, Cheney, Rumsfeld, Wolfowitz etc.) have retired to gated communities to write their self-exonerating memoirs. Assuming that leading a country to war under false pretenses is slightly more grievous than speeding or parking illegally, we still do not insist upon redress, dismissing the fact that any or all of the aforementioned, if traveling in Europe where the verdicts of the World Court mean something, would be summarily arrested like Pinochet and charged as war criminals. We shrug it off, just as we shrug off the actions of President Obama who, despite his good efforts with health care and the automobile industry, has ironically perpetuated and legalized many of the Bush/Cheney policies he campaigned against to be elected. "Politics," we say, and go on about our (but not the nation's) business. And what of the reaction of Catholics when Cardinal Bernard Law of Boston, who was accused of an extended cover-up of deviant priests, was transferred to Rome by John Paul II and, among other appointments, was made a member of a council responsible for the appointment of bishops in the United States? If this wasn't the equivalent of what is corporately called "failing upward," what other name could it have?

By contrast, the rules that govern sports in action are sacrosanct. Almost without exception any violator of the rules is penalized or otherwise made to pay for the transgression. The arbiter is the umpire, referee or another official. His judgment prevails, and there is little room for appeal. The violator may frown, feign innocence or otherwise act like the wronged and not the wronging party, but the call stands. If the violator protests too long or loudly, the umpire can eject him from the game. If he loses control and attacks an umpire or referee, he will find himself heavily fined, suspended or banished from the sport forever.

If respect for the "rules of the game" breaks down, the very integrity of the game deteriorates. Such respect applies not only to players but to officials as well. Years ago when the Russian and American basketball teams competed in the finals of the Olympics, one official extended the conclusion of the game twice until the Russians won. The call was nothing but blatant favoritism. In protest the Americans refused to attend the awards ceremony. They were right to do so.

This sense of fair play is so deeply engrained in our consciences as sports lovers (as players or spectators) that any deviation from the absolute is seen as cheating, whether it be Sammy Sosa's cork-filled bat or doping. What fair-minded lover of baseball, for example, would equate the asterisked records of Bonds, Giambi, McGuire, Sosa and others with those of Ruth, Aaron, DiMaggio or Clemente? We demand fairness with the same passion that we bring to our insistence that every athlete should be judged on his merits as an athlete regardless of race, creed, color, country of origin or anything extraneous to the fact of talent. Not an insignificant insistence...

With the Olympics now upon us, we are brought back to the very birth-place of sports. The poet John Ciardi once wrote: "Sports are human activities made difficult for the joy of it." And the Olympic oath enforces the spirit of that definition: "In the name of all the competitors, I promise that we shall take part in these Olympic games, respecting and abiding by all the rules that govern them, committing ourselves to a sport without doping and without drugs, in the true spirit of sportsmanship, for the glory of sport and the honor of our teams."

Despite the hoopla and the hyper-nationalism, the Olympics attest to the spirit of sports as play—"activities made difficult for the joy of it." Some say it's just a pastime, brief and seasonal and mock-heroic. But pastime or not, it engages the human body, male or female, at its most athletic where unexpectedly a lone player or team may accomplish something no one's ever done as well before. And that endures. What finally matters to the fan though is performance and fairness in competitive, athletic action and absolutely nothing less. The sport-lover wants to witness what the ancient Greek epigram affirmed: "Nothing can take away from a man what he has earned with his hands and his feet." That's what draws us to sports whether the athletes are amateurs or grown men playing boys' games for tycoons' wages.

2011

38

NO TIME FOR POETRY

Why isn't poetry a central presence in our public life? If poetry is human utterance in its most perfect form—felt thought feelingly expressed—, why is it marginalized or overlooked entirely in public speech? The answers to both questions vary in their wrongness.

Some say that poetry is acceptable as long as it is "pleasant," which is like saying that poetry should have the same relationship that Muzak has to music—tolerable as long as it stays soothingly in the background. Others say that poetry should remain at the Hallmark level—the detritus of emotional cliché. Still others point to weddings, funerals and certain honorific events and claim that poetry is often given a place in such proceedings. And this is true. But what passes for poetry then has usually been "written for the occasion." Having heard many of these, I felt that they had been willed (and not inspired) into existence, proving repeatedly that true poems are rarely if ever created on demand.

To cite similar examples in the public domain, consider those times when poets were invited to recite at the presidential inaugurations of Kennedy, Carter, Clinton and Obama—Robert Frost, James Dickey, Maya Angelou, Miller Williams and Elizabeth Alexander. It was fortunate in retrospect that Frost was unable to read the versified treatise he had written for Kennedy's inauguration because the January sun prevented him from seeing the text. Instead (and quite appropriately) he spoke from memory a previously written and infinitely better poem called "The Gift Outright." Dickey and Williams, who are genuine poets by any standard, recited sincerely felt lines that were not in any way comparable to their best work. Maya Angelou simply rhapsodized, and what Elizabeth Alexander recited is best left without comment.

Leaving inaugurations aside, why is it that audiences for "poetry hearings" are spare when compared to those for plays, operas, stand-up comedians or the elaborate noise of rock concerts? Is it because we are a prose-and-screen oriented people who are so inundated daily with advertising copy, journalism, the propaganda of political jargon and gossip that we have no eye or ear for poetry? Is it because noise has hidden poetic values that some of us are missing? Is it simply due to the fact that many poets who read well on the page do not recite well on the stage? Or is it because we have weak attention spans that are not up to what poetry demands? Is this the case in countries other than our own?

Decades ago I was just completing a State Department-sponsored lecture tour to Lebanon, Jordan, Egypt and Greece. In Greece, I met the Nobel poet George Seferis (Georgios

Seferiadis) before his appearance in the Greek Hellenic Union in Athens. Having served the government for much of his life out of Greece, Seferis faced a packed auditorium of people primed to hear their national poet for the first time in his own country. Loudspeakers were set up so that hundreds of people outside the Union could hear him, and thousands heard him in simultaneous broadcast throughout Greece. Such events do not happen in the United States.

But in Greece, the Arab countries and throughout Europe there is a built-in respect for poetic tradition, and this has consequences. Greece is a nation of eleven and half million people, but it has had two Nobel awardees, Seferis and Odysseus Elytis. Ireland, a country of four and a half million, has had three: William Butler Yeats, Samuel Beckett and Seamus Heaney. The United States with a population of three hundred million has had three—T. S. Eliot, Joseph Brodsky and Czeslaw Milosz. Each was a significant poet, although I have retained doubts about Brodsky, but Eliot, though born in St. Louis, emigrated, became an Anglicized American and lived in England all his life. Brodsky and Milosz came from Russia and Poland/Lithuania respectively and wrote in Russian and Polish while here (their work appeared in translation by various hands.) Whatever their merit as poets, none of the three wrote in the American idiom. Allowing for politics on the Nobel committee, were committee members influenced by our indifference to our poets in making their final selections? Why were Robert Frost, Archibald MacLeish, Marianne Moore, Richard Wilbur and Robert Lowell, among others, never considered or chosen?

Perhaps Americans are indifferent to their poets because poets are genuine seers; they write and say what exists beneath appearances without verbiage or deceit. Like the Hebrew prophets they do not write to please. I am speaking here of poets in fact and not in name, not versifiers, tiddly-rhymers, networkers or charlatans.

Jo McDougall's "When the Buck or Two Steakhouse Changed Hands" is so accurate a description of a typical change when something "home-owned" is "franchised" that it deserves to be quoted in its brief entirety: "They put plastic on the menus./They told the waitresses to wear white shoes./They fired Rita./They threw out the unclaimed keys/and the pelican with a toothbrush/that bowed as you left." And what about William Stafford's inserted couplet in "Religion Back Home" that makes us smile before we see all wars from Troy to our present tragic and illegal adventurism in Stafford's semi-playful words: "Our Father Who Art in Heaven/Can lick their Father Who Art in Heaven." And finally there is an indicting couplet by e. e. cummings that is not without merit: "A politician is an arse upon/which everyone has sat except a man."

These are only a handful of examples I have selected to demonstrate the constant relevance of poetry to public life and public speech. The books from which they are drawn are out there and available. And there are thousands of others throughout the world from the time of the Sumerians to right now. If we refuse to read and share them, who can deny that we will be the poorer for it?

2011

39

SAVED BY WIT AND LAUGHTER

IT'S BEEN SAID that one can judge the values of a person or a society by what makes them laugh. Where does America stand? Clown-humor today is passé. Red Skelton, Abbott and Costello, Laurel and Hardy, Sid Caesar and Imogene Coca and even Jerry Lewis stood for mirth. They were in the tradition of clowning that goes back to the court jesters and Pagliacci. Genuine mirth is hardly evident now. In its place have come situation comedies and stand-up comics.

Situation comedies are essentially short-lived episodes that are supposed to parallel what happens with groups or families. The humor derives from scripted action, interplay of characters and laugh-lines. Stand-up comics rely on gags, improvisation, shock and, depending on the medium, the full scale of vulgarity. (I exclude Robin Williams from this conjecture because his comic genius transcended categories.) If protracted, both situation comedies and stand-up monologues turn sour or simply become boring. Both are divorced from the humor of actual life, which happens often by surprise in the course of day-to-day living. It's not an extracurricular activity, not parenthesized in a television time-slot or nightclub act, not a pastime or a luxury. Here are a few examples, public and private, I've plumbed from memory to illustrate the point.

President Roosevelt is said to have defeated Thomas E. Dewey by casting him as the enemy of his dog, Fala. "These Republicans are not satisfied with attacking me, my wife and my sons, but even my dog, Fala. Now I and my wife and my sons don't mind, but my dog, Fala, does mind. In fact he hasn't been the same dog since."

In a later decade Senator Everett Dirksen was speaking in the Senate while another elderly senator was seated in front of him and loudly chewing, snapping and popping bubblegum. Dirksen became noticeably irritated, paused, stared at the senator and said in his mellifluent basso, "You, sir, are a masticating sexegenarian."

After an impeached Bill Clinton faced conviction because of the Lewinsky scandal, it actually was an eleventh hour speech by Senator Dale Bumpers of Arkansas that stymied the righteousness of Clinton's accusers. "This reminds me," said Bumpers, "of a parish meeting in rural Arkansas. A minister asked his parishioners if they knew anyone as perfect as our Lord and Savior Jesus Christ. There was no answer, so he asked again if anyone had ever heard of someone as perfect as our Lord and Savior Jesus Christ. One man held up his hand and said he knew of one....his wife's first husband."

A friend of mine told a similar story when he had to return to Pittsburgh for family reasons. To lighten the mood he recounted the tale of an Irish priest who had to speak at the wake of a parishioner he did not know. He asked other parishioners to tell him some good things the deceased had done so that he could include them in his eulogy. There was no response. "You mean you can't think of one good thing this man did!" One parishioner said, "His brother was worse."

Recently I viewed a U-Tube video from Tel Aviv created by an Israeli satirist and comedian. It consisted of a series of excerpts from the recent speech of Benjamin Netanyahu to Congress. Each excerpt featured one line from the speech followed by a wide shot of members of Congress leaping to their feet and applauding wildly. There were about twenty or more of these excerpts followed by the audience members jumping to their feet as if on cue and clapping. The Israeli comedian was pictured in a sidebar throughout, and he was laughing harder and harder as one excerpt followed another. He seemed to be finding the whole episode hilarious. What many Americans have since considered a servile, shameful and even obsequious exhibition by our elected officials struck this comedian as a sideshow or as something left over from vaudeville. No American satirist or otherwise has yet exposed this ludicrous and demeaning episode as well or better than this one Israeli.

I remember two incidents that happened during my years at Duquesne that are unforgettable. Robert Beranek was an excellent professor of Political Science. Even on the coldest days he never wore an overcoat. Sometimes he went outdoors in shirtsleeves. When asked why he didn't bundle up, he would say dismissively, "I do not participate in winter." When told that he was risking his health, he would repeat, "I do not participate."

The Dean of the School of Business Administration at one time was Dr. Clarence Walton, who later became the President of Catholic University. He made a daily commute to his office in the Fitzsimons Building in town and then walked up to his first class on the bluff. One time he arrived at his classroom early, realized he had left some student papers in his downtown office and walked down to get them before returning to the classroom. He was ten minutes late for the class, and the students had legitimately left. He was livid. When the class met next, he said, "Last Monday I was late because I had gone to retrieve your test papers, and you did not have the courtesy to wait a few minutes longer for me. I left my coat here. When my coat is here, I'm here." At the subsequent class there were no students, but there was a coat at each chair.

In domestic life there are little instances of humor that occur without fanfare or rehearsal. My eight-year-old granddaughter said to me recently, "Poppo, today is Friday, but sometimes it's Wednesday."

A mother I know was watching a televised weather report with her grade-school son. At one point he nudged her and asked, "Why is it always ten degrees colder in the windshield factory?"

One of the assets of humor—real humor—is that it clears the air. It brings us back to the world as it is. It does not mean that we take life any less seriously than it deserves. It only means that the absence of indispensable humor in our lives is something we should take seriously. We need it.

2015

40

HOW SWEET THE SOUND

MANY PEOPLE THINK that poetry is nothing more than language that "sounds nice." Nothing could be further from the truth. Unlike so much Hallmark and Swinburnian drivel, poems are not written to please. Poets write compulsively to re-create their visions and feelings in words (in their literal, suggestive, symbolic and tonal dimensions) so that those who hear or read them can see and feel them as well. For example, it's one thing to state that genuine love is unforgettable. But it's something else to say this as piercingly as John Donne said it four centuries ago: "*I cannot say I loved, for who can say/He was killed yesterday?*" Similarly the contemporary poet Richard Wilbur wrote two-lines of light verse for and with his children that cannot be easily dismissed as something exclusively for children: "*What is the opposite of two?/A lonely me, a lonely you.*"

If we assume that poetry is nothing but nice sounds, there's a lot of phony poetry out there that qualifies. It presents us with imagination at the service of groupthink, subliminal persuasion or mellifluence to "con" the public by using various poetic tropes and techniques but not for poetic purposes.

The poet William Matthews once said that "Advertising is the poetry of capitalism." And he's correct. What, for example, makes Lexus' *"passionate pursuit of perfection"* memorable but its alliterative "p's"? And there's an echo of the same technique in "*My choice, my money, Meineke.*" And some of us may remember Dinah Shore's anthem at the conclusion of her television show: *"See the USA/In your Chevrolet!"* Such examples are omnipresent in speech or print, and they all follow the same formula—"sound-bites" to promote a product. The purpose? Enticing the potential buyer. The goal? Sales.

And then we have the Pentagon poets. They give patriotic, noble and even biblical names to lethal ventures. Behind the moniker of *Operation Iraqi Freedom* (now mutated into *Operation New Dawn*), which had nothing to do with freedom at all, were the military and civilian deathcounts (in the thousands for us, and the tens and hundreds of thousands for "them.") *There was Operation All-American Tiger* that designated the search for Saddam Hussein's cronies. There was *Operation Odyssey Dawn* to upgrade our questionably legal "lead from the rear" attacks in Libya. During the Korean War General Matthew Ridgway pursued *Operation Killer* and *Operation Ripper*, but he was reprimanded for using both names because they actually matched their intentions. Sweet-sounding and uplifting titles were preferred and have been obligatory since to hide war's true nature. War won't "sell" to the public unless it's made to sound redemptive.

Poetic sloganeering has long been used in politics to elect or at least try to define a candidate. "*I Like Ike*" was probably the most memorable, but there was also "*All the Way with LBJ*" and "*Be Clean for Gene.* "And the Reagan boosters settled for "*It's Morning Again in America.*" By the time it was afternoon we had lost more than 240 Marines south of Beirut because the administration would not permit the Marines on post to have their weapons loaded. Then we had Iran Contra with the forgettably unforgettable Colonel Oliver North and, later, Casper Weinberger, both of whom, unlike today where malefactors are not even charged, were presidentially pardoned. And finally we had a tripling of the annual deficit and an increase of the national debt from 995 billion to 2.9 trillion.

Speaking of money, the very names of the new PAC's that are now legally absolved from hiding or otherwise disguising themselves from public scrutiny (thanks to a 5-4 ruling from the current Supreme Court) take the buying of elections to a new level. They indirectly bankroll candidates of their choice, and the sky's the limit. But they have names that sound as inspiring as titles for themes in a beginner's course in Civics: *Restore Our Future, American Crossroads, Winning Our Future, Make Us Great Again, Priorities USA Action, Endure Liberty, Our Destiny* and *Red, White and Blue Fund.* This is all palpable bilge that simply turns elections into costly rivalries between advertising agencies with candidates propped or puppeteered like endmen in a minstrel show.

And what about the nominal code-words that tap our hidden preferences for certain cars. A Ford V8 was name enough at one time. Now sub-names add to the allure: *Monte Carlo,*

Eldorado, Riviera, Maxima, Optima, Legend, Avalon, Escalade, Rendezvous etc. No car has the sub-name of Hamtramck or Lower Burrell. Years ago Henry Ford II asked the renowned poet Marianne Moore to come up with a name for a new model to be added to the Ford line. Some of her nominations included *Thundercrester, Silver Bullet, Varsity Stroke, Mongoose Civic, Turcotinga* and *Pastelogram*. They were all deservedly rejected (Ms. Moore's talent did not transfer well to advertising copy) in favor of the first name of the elder Ford's son, Edsel. It didn't last.

Finally there are names given to public or ecclesiastical officials that seem more rhapsodic than necessary, as in *The Most Honorable, The Most* or *The Very Reverend, Your Grace, Your Royal Highness, Your Holiness, Your Majesty* and other hyperboles. However sincere they may sound or seem on the page, they have the odor of social elevation about them without the sealevel scent of humanity. Where did this start? What in the final judgment is more honest and poetic than a proper name and what the owner of that name made of it?

One thinks of Harry S. Truman who, at the end of his term, drove with his wife in his own car without Secret Service protection from Washington, D. C. to Independence, Missouri. He had a military pension of $1,350.72 per year, and that was all until Congress voted him a modest supplement. When offered corporate appointments, he declined, claiming that this would be trading on his presidency, which he thought did not belong to him but to the people. He also declined to accept the Congressional Medal of Honor in the same spirit. His prime asset at death was the house he lived in, which his wife had inherited from her mother. This contrasts markedly with the after-office lives of recent holders of the presidency who accept and welcome honoraria in the millions or live lives of private opulence in gated communities or penthouses and appear with great ceremony to open multi-million dollar libraries named after them or the like. One can differ with some or many of the policies and actions initiated by Truman as President (and I do), but it is difficult to find fault with his deportment thereafter. In some ways it's reminiscent of the post-Presidential actions of Thomas Jefferson. Asked what he wanted to be remembered for, Jefferson specified only three things: author of the Declaration of Independence, framer of Virginia's Statutes on Religious Freedom, and Founder of the University of Virginia. These are on his tombstone. There's no mention of his presidency, which he called a "splendid misery."

2014

41

THE ART OF BEING COMPLETE

In 1927 Charles Lindbergh flew non-stop from Long Island to Paris in just under thirty-four hours. This was less than two and a half decades after the Wright brothers made the first manned and motor-driven flight, which lasted a bit more than twelve seconds. That kind of advancement in aeronautics burgeoned throughout the twentieth century as airplanes were used for warfare, postal and cargo delivery, recreation, transportation of passengers from city to city as well as from continent to continent. This has always affirmed for me that aeronautical science, as well as every other science, is a work in progress. New inventions and technological discoveries invariably open new scientific frontiers in flight, surgery, telecommunications or architecture.

This is not the case with the arts. Every work of art is created *complete* whether it be a poem, a song, a play, a painting or a sculpture. Shakespeare's ROMEO AND JULIET was and is and will always be one of a kind—a work pristine and inimitable. The same holds true for Michelangelo's DAVID, Maurice

Ravel's BOLERO and Robert Frost's "The Road Not Taken." All of these were created just once in their entirety and endure in an eternal present because people who read, hear or see them find them unforgettable and return to them again and again. Always themselves in their original perfection, they outlive and continue to outlive the times and places of their creation.

This suggests to me that the essential difference between science and the arts is the difference between *progress* and *perpetuity*. There is no question that most Americans prefer progress. Technology (applied science) serves multiple purposes and is always being updated. The new succeeds the old, and we Americans, as a matter of habit, opt for novelty. The arts offer something entirely different—something made by head, heart and hand in perpetuity and beyond further improvement once completed.

Consider poetry as an example. No matter who the author might be, a genuine poem stops us in our tracks, and we remember it because we simply can't forget it. Without such experiences in our lives we simply become historical creatures, even though something in us yearns for moments that will outlive the present. Poetry, as well as the other arts, is capable of giving us those moments.

Of course, much of what passes for poetry today in public life is not poetry at all. Mawkish Hallmark jingles are not poetry but sentimentality versified. And what appears in many magazines and journals, i.e. THE NEW YORKER, POETRY and THE ATLANTIC under their current editors, sounds as if the writers all went to the same clique-ish workshop. Their poems read like messages from pen pals to pen pals. There is strong dependence on typography while others who write solely out of ethnicity, race or gender create nothing but sociology without imagination. The annual award juries, looking for another Ashbery or someone equally shallow and indecipherable, do nothing to correct the record. Similarly, poems written on demand, like those heard at recent presidential inaugurals, make us wonder who did the choosing, and why.

Another reason for poetry's being disregarded by the public at large is that many poets who say their poems in public do so as if the poem were just a page in the telephone directory. Ideally, poetry readings should actually be recitals. Poets who are totally dependent on their books at the rostrum are like actors who are still holding their scripts in their hands during a performance. The drama evaporates. The printed poem can best be compared to sheet music, which does not become music until it's heard. Once a poet has committed his poems to memory and can recite them directly to the eyes of his listeners—only then does the poem come to life.

Ezra Pound once said (correctly) that all poetry is contemporary, and this is true since poetry's subject matter is whatever is timeless in the human heart and spirit. Good poems are available in libraries and public bookstores and even on the air, thanks to Garrison Keillor's ALMANACK. To its great credit the PITTSBURGH POST-GAZETTE for two decades has prominently published a weekly poem on its editorial pages and still does. In other words, poems are there for the reading or listening if we take the time to read or listen. But we don't.

Almost all that we read or hear daily is prose—advertising, government or legal jargon, newspaper and magazine writing, gossip and the like. Most of it is eminently forgettable. If you doubt that, try to think of a single phrase or statement—just one—you have read or heard over the last two days that you cannot forget.

Those who live exclusively by the clock and calendar rarely make time for poetic moments that help us define and transcend our circumstances. Poetry and the other arts offer this gratis in perpetuity. If we open ourselves to them, we will be rewarded tenfold and share in the everlasting *now* that is art. We will then find ourselves living with ongoing presences. And ongoing presences have no past tense.

2015

42

THE TIMELESS IS ALWAYS TIMELY

MORE OFTEN THAN NOT, commencement speeches, which are now in the offing, tend to rank high in the romantic literature of our time. Congratulatory or tamely optimistic, they rarely reinforce what most college bulletins promise—an education that strengthens critical thinking, written and oral competence, cultural awareness and some grounding in the sciences and fine arts. What does this mean? One thing it means is that graduates should possess *minds*, not merely *trained intelligences*. They should not be gullible—not quick to believe the party line in social affairs, political action, educational policy or doctrinaire religious questions, particularly of the fundamentalist variety. As students of history they should at least have developed a historical sense, which means understanding the past origins of present-day problems. In our time it should alert them to see that any nation or group that attempts to impose its will by force on another nation or group is courting its own degeneration. "Who overcomes by force," wrote Milton, "hath overcome but half his foe."

With regard to those who equate power with weapons or money, they should ask if anyone would pay any attention to them if they were unarmed or broke. As Arthur Miller has one of his characters say of J. P. Morgan in DEATH OF A SALESMAN, "In a Turkish bath he looked like a butcher, but with his pockets on he was very well liked."

As students of matters spiritual, they should recognize that people of genuine spirituality need no rationale for their belief and that theology, as one brilliant theologian stated, is often the philosophy of the unbeliever. This is why they should be immediately suspicious of fundamentalists of any creed who think they are prophetic and act as if the Renaissance had never happened. Such primitives rarely question, and invariably they tend to speak in pronouncements. It's the "You're with or against us mentality," which is a mentality of absolute answers but no questions.

If a collegiate education has deepened an appreciation of music in graduates (even though they may not have the talent to be musicians themselves), they should work to keep that talent alive and growing. What passes for popular music today—electronically amplified, spotlighted and smoke-enhanced in performance—has as much relation to music as mud-wrestling has to gymnastics.

And as students of the American language, graduates should sense instinctively when it is misused or abused. This is especially relevant in their estimate of those in public whose voices are frequently heard or whose words are frequently read. They can judge such people by a simple test. Imagine each of them in front of a class of students (since students can tell the real thing from a fraud in a matter of minutes), and then make up their minds about them. Above all, they should remember that the purpose of language is to reveal as clearly and feelingly as possible what is in the mind and heart. Anything less is nothing but the merchandising of language for lesser purposes. Those who talk much and say little should remind them of the old adage—"The bigger the mouth, the smaller the mind." But those who speak and write well—those whose language can be trusted emotionally and intellectually—should be their role models for the word. These people create, in the words of John Bayley, "the inevitable solace that right language brings." This is not on a par with ordering a hamburger from McDonald's or bargaining with a used car salesman.

When we speak or write our best, we come as close as possible to immortality. We are capable at such times of doing something with words that will outlive us. This is not a matter of vanity or vainglory. Had Abraham Lincoln uttered but a few clichés at Gettysburg, no one would remember them. But he spoke in the space of scarcely three minutes just two hundred and seventy-two words (barely three-fourths of one typewritten or printed sheet of paper) to define what America meant and still means, and those words will live, not merely a print or in bronze, but in our hearts and minds as long as political freedom means anything in this world. And I could say similar things about Shakespeare and any number of other writers. They left words that have outlived them and will in fact keep them alive as long as people hear or read them. Despite all that we hear about literacy and as important as literacy is to a functioning democracy, what we truly expect from college graduates and lifelong learners is fluency—the art of choosing words that say as faithfully as possible what they mean. As Ted Sorensen has written, "The less often that Americans hear thoughtful public discourse, the more likely they are to be vulnerable to deceptive demagoguery… Stirring phrases have been replaced by soundbites and applause lines."

If measuring up to standards like these makes college graduates different, so be it. They did not go to college just to blend with the scenery, and they do not leave college to blend with the scenery to come. Their words should always do justice to the world, regardless of the reactions they might provoke. And they should try to be as terse as possible. When Shakespeare has Polonius say that "brevity is the soul of wit," he was really speaking of more than wit. Brevity is the soul of genuine utterance. It has intensity, and intensity has power that is unignorable. It's like sunlight focused through a magnifying glass. It can set things ablaze. It infuses a statement like this one made by President Franklin D. Roosevelt: "The measure of our greatness will not be whether we gave more to those who have much but whether we gave enough to those who have little." And what about the force of this aphorism: "The silence of the envious is too noisy." And finally there is a statement that my then ten-year-old grandson said to his mother after she had helped him with his arithmetic for more than an hour—"Mom, I'll love you to the last number."

These are but three examples chosen at random that go beyond mere verbiage. But they stick in the mind. Each one sounds as final as a car door being shut but perfect as a telegram to God.

2013

43

NOT RIGHT BUT SO

ALL OF US NEED CERTAINTIES in our lives. But too often we come to accept what is incorrect or ambiguous as substitutes for certainty. We learn to live with these substitutes either because we can't change or refute them or because we don't recognize them as wrong in the first place.

Take the months of September, October, November and December, for example. Judging only from their prefixes (sept, oct, novem and decem), they should be the seventh, eighth, ninth and tenth months of the year. But they are posted on our calendars as the ninth, tenth, eleventh and twelfth. Why? Because Julius Caesar and Augustus Caesar wanted their names enshrined on two of the months of the year. Hence July and August. And September, October, November and December were moved down and out of order to make room.

The same concession to power explains the Castilian accent in Spanish in which the letters "c" and "d" are often pronounced as "th." *Paciencia* is so-spelled, but it is pronounced Castilianly as "*pathienthia*." Why? Because a prominent member of the royal family lisped (or rather *lithped*).

In France it's a matter of law that the twin born last is considered the older. When I mentioned to one Frenchman that this did not make sense, he shrugged and said, "Tant pis" ("So what?"). And that was that.

Thus far, three "wrongs," and they are ongoing and probably will remain ongoing.

We also tend to accept phrases that are really sham descriptions of reality. Consider the phrase "senseless murder," for example. The implication apparently is that there should be "sensible murders," which leads us away from the noun and focuses on the misleading adjective, which tries but fails to make sense of killings as if such acts can always be rationally explainable.

The phrase "untimely death" is often used to lament the death of the young. But any doctor or philosopher will tell you that death has no birthday and that deaths by disease or violence happen when they happen, regardless of age. What might seem untimely to the survivors is nothing but the random unfairness of life as usual, untimely or not.

And, of course, there is the blatant and rationalized wrongness of the fraudulent war in Iraq. This was originally called a crusade, then a war against terror, then a way of transplanting democracy in the Middle East and so on. Countless books and articles have by now contradicted these incorrect and blatant descriptions of a war concocted by a cabal of fearless neo-conservatives together with Vice-President Cheney.

Now the Iraq war's original wrongness has been superceded by the mantra of "nation building." No one has raised the analogy that the only way to correct going the wrong way down a one-way street is to stop. Our definition of stopping means to hunker down and stay, regardless of all the talk of withdrawal and free elections etc. Not right but so.

Based on these facts, how is it possible to reconcile the deaths of more than 4,000 service personnel, the wounding of more than 31,000, the suffering caused by Post Traumatic Stress Disorder and depression of 300,000 veterans (these are not my figures but those given by the Rand Corporation,) plus the deaths and injuries sustained by more than 1,000,000 Iraqis? And how does one respond to the ongoing reports of suicides among these same troops either while on duty or after returning to their families? Recently the military high command, which shares with government a total reluctance to accuse itself of error, reported that there were 128 soldier suicides in 2008, which was an increase over the previous year's total of 117. Military officials consider suicides only those deaths caused by gun, knife or noose. Drug overdoses are identified as accidents as are automobile wrecks or collisions attributable to alcoholism. Under a headline claiming that the government lied about suicide figures, Senator Patty Murray of Washington, while investigating this question, discovered that the Veterans Administration calculated that there were 12,000 suicide attempts in 2008, though the army counterclaimed that there were only (only!) 800, and that the actual suicide count was in the multi hundreds.

As if these figures are not sobering enough, CBS conducted its own investigations years earlier and discovered that 6,256 veterans who had served in Iraq and Afghanistan committed suicide in 2005 alone. This was subsequently corroborated by the Army's own Suicide Event Report that confirmed, without citing specific figures, that the 2005 suicide rate among veterans was the highest it had been in 26 years, particularly true among soldiers who had served in multiple deployments. Later, *Democracy Now* (PBS) and MSNBC confirmed this figure and stated at the time that an additional 5,000 veterans were expected to take their lives in 2006. If accurate, these figures are staggering.

Whom does one believe? Where does one go for certainty? I spoke to several friends in government service. They could not and would not speak on the record, but they did not dispute or contradict the aforementioned figures. They did note, however, that the number of homeless veterans had become an endemic national problem and that there were 1500 homeless vets in Allegheny County alone. Trying to find parallel situations and figures, I wondered if veterans of the Vietnam War had a similar history, heretofore unreported, and learned that the suicide rate among such veterans from the time of the end of the war until 1983 was only slightly less than those killed in the war itself, approximately 58,000. Robert Filner, Chairman of the Congressional Veterans Affairs Committee, claimed in 2007 that the figure then actually exceeded 58,000. Authors Chuck Dean (*Nam Vet*) and Alexander Paul (*Suicide Wall*) confirm this, adding that self-destructive behavior among veterans after the war ended was fairly widespread but under-reported.

It's no formula for one's peace of mind to discover things that are not right but so. What are the options? One can keep silent or just go along, as many did through much of this decade, but that literally condoned what should not have been happening. Or one can dissent as millions around the world did when Bush, now one of the more prominent creators of unnecessary funerals in Presidential history, "decided" on a policy of war without end. Although dissent was ignored or branded as unpatriotic, we know now the price paid in lives lost or maimed. If the dead could speak, which option would they have supported?

2011

44

AND GLADLY TEACH

APPARENTLY IT'S OPEN SEASON on teachers. The dogmatized, rhyming governors of Wisconsin, Indiana, Ohio, New Jersey and our own Pennsylvania have made it their mission to discipline and reform the teaching profession in the name of fiscal sanity. Why? The given reason is that the state treasuries, in order to remain solvent, need the money that would normally be spent on teachers' salaries and benefits. This is the justification that usually translates as the "bottom line" in such matters. What's left unsaid is that there is a top line which identifies teaching as an essential and indispensable human service performed by professionals, without which the bottom line would not exist. Such professionals are as deserving of respect and a just remuneration as are doctors, dentists, judges or, for that matter, governors.

Instead, the teaching profession is berated, particularly by those who never taught and who could not win the respect of students if they did. So they dredge up the old clichés – "Those who can do; those who can't teach." They say that teachers work short hours in a ten-month year and are spoiled baby boomers. Such critics do not need a refutation as much as they need an education. They have the same mentality as the Bush administration dolts who conceived the "No Child Left Behind" folly, in which students were not educated for self-discovery and prepared for further study but simply trained to score well on standardized tests.

Teaching in essence combines both the conservative and liberal aspects of learning by preserving what is valuable and eternally relevant from the past and sharing it with others in the present. In this spirit someone once rightly defined education as a period when students are absented from the present for a time in order to learn from the past so that they can better face the present in the future. Ideally all students should embody the spirit of the student-clerk in Chaucer's CANTERBURY TALES – "and gladly would he learn and gladly teach." Since all teachers are in fact but older students, they should personify and perpetuate this spirit all their lives (as most good teachers do, without a doubt). For them teaching is what a great educator like Gilbert Highet called it – an art. And the best teachers are those who, in addition to and over and above their professional qualifications, not only know what they are talking about but have the good of their students at heart. The students who benefit are forever grateful.

Listening to the patronizing remarks of Governor Robert Walker of Wisconsin was to be left with the impression that he regarded teachers as house servants whose status and rights would be determined by the head of the house, namely, himself. Surely he and his similarly motivated governor-colleagues know that the war-drain (pre-Libya) on the federal government is what had dried up social and infrastructure federal assistance to the states, some of which would certainly have been ticketed for education. And they know as well that the corporations that are in lock-step with them (and contributed to their campaigns) have benefited mightily from no-bid contracts that the former administration gave them to re-construct what we had destroyed in Iraq and Afghanistan. (For the full story of this collusion I refer you to Naomi Klein's THE SHOCK DOCTRINE.) But instead of going after the war-lovers and the war-profiteers, these governors are going after, among others, teachers.

In a country where student rankings in science and math are at the 17th and 12th level respectively and where the United States is ranked 12th in college graduation, what savants except the governors themselves believe that reducing the salaries and benefits of teachers, enlarging class size and letting some teachers go would improve the situation? If this is the meaning of fiscal sanity, what is fiscal insanity?

The wars in which we have been involved since 2003 (Afghanistan and Iraq) have been universally called illegal and unwinnable. The almost papal pronouncements of General Petraeus have not changed legal minds in this regard. And the ongoing costs of continuance are astronomical. Here are the specifics, and the figures are conservative. Exclusive of Libya (called operation ODYSSEY DAWN by the poets in the Pentagon), war costs come to $5,000 per second. That amounts to $300,000 per minute. This adds up to $18,000,000 an hour, which means $432,000,000 a day. One year's total is $157,680,000,000. That's one hundred and fifty-seven billion six hundred and eighty million bucks, Mr. and Mrs. America, every year! The combined cost of eight years of war is $1,261,440,000,000. That is almost the equivalent of the current deficit. And war money, let us remember, is money down the drain. Here is a parallel in civilian terms. The annual budget of the University of Pittsburgh, including the medical schools, is approximately $2,000,000,000. That amount would fund the ongoing, feckless and illegal wars in Iraq and Afghanistan for not quite five days!

Anyone who can add can see that the wealth of the country is being disproportionately divided and that at-home expenses are being given the bottom of the barrel, if that. If the governors of the several states see that their treasuries are in decline because the costs of federal adventurism are taking away money that should rightly have come to them, they should forthrightly place the blame where it belongs, namely, on the President and the Congress. They are the primary ones in position to reverse or otherwise modify a policy that is having debilitating effects on the country.

It certainly makes no sense to impose the burden of budget-balancing on teachers under whose tutelage the future of the country depends. It's been said that fighting for the rights of others is really fighting for one's own rights since human rights are common to us all. Supporting teachers whose rights to bargain collectively for just wages and benefits have been quite arbitrarily jeopardized or suspended is as good a place to start as any. And the time to start is yesterday.

2014

45

CUTTING HEIGHT DOWN TO SIZE

MANY WHO WILL READ these comments will find them unrealistic, irrelevant, controversial and possibly annoying, and they will be right. But I mean and stand by every word.

Basically I have a problem accepting phoney illusions of height—in architecture, in myth, in belief, in social life, in motion. Take, for example, the calendar art or photography that is intended to extol and promote New York, Dallas, Boston or Pittsburgh. Featured always are downtown sections with tall buildings front and center. Excluded are a fountain in a park, neighborhood streets, an elementary school or an occasional bridge. Leaving aside the obvious promotional and commercial reasons for featuring downtown sections, whoever said that tall buildings deserve such focus? After all, what are buildings with umpteen stories but a realtor's ploy for maximum profit under the glow of a poetic device known as a kenning—"skyscraper." The game is to rent or sell every space at ground level, then replicate the process by building a second story on top of the first. After renting or selling all the space on the second floor, build a third story and keep going up and up until you "scrape the sky." This marriage of architecture and entrepreneurism and the genius of James Otis, who invented the safety elevator, has been the formula for creating downtowns ever since.

Presently under construction in Manhattan is an eighty-four story skyscraper that will offer for sale eighty-some luxury apartments pancaked on top of one another. I have no doubt that the building will be totally occupied in short order. But what's the attraction? Status? The view? A handy downtown *pied a terre*? An income tax deduction? I find myself wondering if the upper floor or penthouse dwellers will regard the daily ascent or descent by elevator as anything but boring. And since elevators can and do stall at times, I wonder if such a breakdown ever occurs to them as a possibility. If you've ever had the pleasure of being trapped in a stalled, crowded elevator with no lights, it's not an event that you forget easily or ever. And what about the warnings from firemen that the rescue of tenants above the seventh floor in burning buildings is difficult to impossible. The horrific destruction of the Twin Towers revealed that in all its horror when rescue of those in the upper floors was hopeless from the start.

Height also figures into power structures. Why do corporations and other institutions, including some universities, locate the offices of chief executive officers or presidents on top floors? Is this a way of rewarding corporate ascent, of demonstrating that some have reached the "top rung of the ladder," of showing that those "in power" have floors of lesser fry "under them?"

In a different but still related vein, what is it that motivates adventurers to climb Everest or the Matterhorn or some random alp chosen for conquest? I realize that such feats demonstrate "what man can do," but to what purpose beyond inner satisfaction or the side benefits generated by publicity? What benefits to humanity accrue from their efforts?

Mountains also figure into matters of belief. It was once believed that gods dwelt on or near Olympus and the Himalayas. In the Judeo-Christian tradition it is related in the Old Testament that Moses received the Commandments from God on Mt. Sinai. But at best isn't this only mythology? Pagans and early believers somehow venerated gods of their own creation and imagined them on mountain heights or in the "heavens." It was their supra-terrestrial way of lifting them above and beyond sealevel life. Putting God in the stratosphere ("the heavens") seemed an acceptable locale. Perhaps that is why people in prayer are described as "raising their eyes to God," or why survivors often speak of deceased loved ones as always "looking down on them." Or why Irving Berlin in what is now regarded as our second national anthem wrote of being guided "with the light from above." And what of all other ascensions (ascended where?) or assumptions (assumed where?). More mythology, of course. Christ who, as a Jew and a savior, bridges both testaments and should presumably be regarded as an authority on the subject gave heaven its exact address just once when He said, "The kingdom of heaven is within you" and nowhere else.

He could have added that the kingdom of hell is within as well. Omar Khayyam said as much centuries later in "The Rubaiyat" ("I myself am heaven and hell"), and I for one think he had a point.

The illusions of height are all-pervasive. We say, for example, that certain people are elevated to "high office" or that others, by virtue of birth alone and not character or accomplishment, must be addressed as Highness and should have their "exalted presence" honored with a bow. Nonsense, but we comply.

None of this will change, of course. We perpetuate rather than reform because compliance is simpler, and tradition is on the side of compliance. Consider the phrase "high speed" when applied to motion. Pilots are lauded for breaking the sound barrier, and racing drivers and itinerant law-breakers think nothing of exceeding one hundred miles per hour. The facts are that it is the plane or vehicle that is doing the speeding. Pilots and drivers are sitting stock-still in a cockpit or driver's seat and are being sped.

2014

46

WHAT'S REALLY IN A NAME?

NAME-GIVERS. THAT'S WHAT WE ARE. By necessity, choice or compulsion we name our children, our streets, our neighborhoods, our cities, our states and so on. Biblical literalists trace this to Genesis where Adam was commanded by God to give a name to everything in Eden. Others simply acknowledge that giving names to things is our way of knowing the world. In other words, if we can name it, we know it.

Historically the world into which we are born has to a great extent already been named by our predecessors. From kindergarten to college and beyond what passes for education means learning names. In the course of our education we often conclude that many of these already given names are ones we are stuck with. By tradition, usage and agreement they rightly stand for what they designate, but they frequently leave room for improvement. Surely someone could have used more imagination before coming up with "fireplace" or "bedroom." Such words mean what they stand for, but they do it in the most prosaic way possible. They evoke nothing. On the other hand there are words that match their dictionary meanings by their very sounds. What sounds more conniving than "treachery," more thief-like and underhanded than "embezzle," more lethal than the two flat, whole notes in "murder?"

It is a challenge to the poet in each of us to find or give names to things or conditions that go beyond dictionary definitions, that evoke the very nature of what the name stands for. If this means re-naming things, so be it. Poems are often nothing more than searches for the right word or words that feelingly define a moment, an object, a sensation or a felt thought. In the dawn of the English language the earliest poets or scops invented words like "battleflash" to describe a sword, or they would identify a boat by its function with a kenning like "wave-skimmer." These images evoked a deeper connection between words and the world as it truly is. And when these poets and their successors wrote of personal matters, one sensed a real connection between their words and what was in their minds and hearts, as in Robert Browning's "A man's reach should exceed his grasp, or what's a heaven for?" Or what Shakespeare has Hamlet whisper as he faces death, "The rest is silence."

Regrettably, there are many forces in society that stand opposed to the difficult task of naming things rightly. In polite terms this is called diplomacy, tact, euphemism or political correctness. Its real name is hypocrisy or naked lying. And it can have lethal consequences. In Nazi Germany Joseph Goebbels was a master at such duplicity. The condemned entered

Auschwitz under the welcoming banner—"Arbeit Macht Frei" (Work Makes Free). The only freedom that awaited them was starvation or incineration. In our own recent history we have the "No Child Left Behind" program. It sounds fine, but in fact it provides for rewarding teachers for training students to garner high test scores in specific subjects. In return for facilitating an improvement in student test scores, the teachers are rewarded with raises. In fact this is simply bribery academic-style, and the valuable thing that is really left behind is what used to be called a complete education. In matters of foreign policy we have been euphemized to the point of saturation with "New Europe versus Old Europe," "Operation Iraqi Freedom," "Mission Accomplished," "The Birth of a New Middle East," "Axis of Evil" and other consequences of "Compassionate Conservatism." All of these are false. If I. F. Stone and George Orwell were alive today, they would greet such rot with an I-told-you-so smile or a smirk of total exasperation.

A friend of mine told me years ago that he read poetry because it cleaned up his act. This is hardly a scholarly definition, but it makes its point. We all hunger for the truth, even when it's disconcerting. But people numbed by propagandists often to their regret settle for phoniness. After all, the probity of our deepest thoughts and feelings does not surface easily. It frequently takes a poet to say what we would very much like to say. Matthew Arnold concludes "Dover Beach" with these lines: "And we are here as on a darkling plain/Where ignorant armies clash by night." In those few words we see every war of the twentieth century plus the current one. When Robert

Lowell described traffic in downtown Boston, he wrote that "a savage servility/slides by on grease." Was he speaking only of traffic? And then there is William Blake"s famous couplet: "We are led to believe a lie/When we see not through but with the eye." Seeing through the eye was undoubtedly what prompted Norman Mailer to describe the segregationist former Governor of Georgia Lester Maddox, who passed out axe handles to his followers to "discourage" certain voters from voting, as having "the face of a mean baby with glasses on it." And what of Naomi Shihab Nye who wrote of a distant uncle that he was "famous for his laugh." And suddenly the uncle is right there, totally sketched in a single sentence.

2010

47

SPIEL VERSUS SPEECH

WHO WAS IT said that advertising is the poetry of capitalism? Regardless of attribution, the indebtednesss of advertising to poetry presents a few superficial crossovers, frequent borrowings as well as some essential differences.

First, the crossovers and borrowings. Advertising, like poetry, relies heavily on images. Advertising, like poetry, depends for its effect on a quick impact. Advertising, like poetry, is frequently reliant upon mnemonics (memory-aiding tokens or techniques) to facilitate and encourage remembrance. Advertising, like poetry, often allies itself with rhythm and rhyme—occasionally to the accompaniment of music—to achieve its maximum effect.

Now, the essential differences, beginning with imagery. The image in poetry is rooted in inspiration itself, as in Shakespeare's aside about jealousy—"It is the green-eyed monster that mocks the meat it feeds on." Poets by nature think not in concepts but images, which can best be described as sensations in language.

Advertising's reliance on brevity of expression or a quick focus is almost synonymous with advertising itself. Part of this, of course, is due to cost. Thirty or sixty seconds of television advertising can run into millions. A full page of advertising in the NEW YORK TIMES is roughly equivalent to the sticker price of a fully equipped Mercedes Benz. But the compelling reason for conciseness in advertising is to capture the roving attention of the potential consumer in a flash fix or byte before he is distracted.

Because remembering what has been advertised is the ultimate purpose of any spiel or pitch, advertisers use a variety of mnemonics. Automobile ads, for example, concentrate on logos—the Cadillac harp, the L of the Lexus, the Honda H and so forth. Other mnemonics like Chevrolet's "like a rock," the AFLAC talking gander or the YUK image on medicine bottles serve the same purpose.

Because rhythm can usurp our attention whether we are fully aware of it or not, advertisers write or speak rhythmically (even with occasional rhyme) whenever possible. The original Pepsi-Cola commercial was the father of this tradition: "Pepsi-Cola hits the spot. Twelve full ounces, that's a lot. Twice as much for a nickel too. Pepsi-Cola is the drink for you." The nickel price obviously dates this commercial, but the reliance on rhythm and rhyme is unmistakable. Its imitators include Mazda's "zoom, zoom, zoom" repeated ad nauseam and the alliterative "Bush's Best Baked Beans."

Why are these tropes of prosody attractive to advertisers? The answer is that imagery, lyrical brevity, mnemonic aids, rhythm and rhyme have the capacity to engage and focus our attention. They draw us into the present tense and keep us there as long as our attention is so entranced and concentrated. At such times we are more or less at the mercy of the moment. If the moment is truly poetic, it can alter our perceptions and create feelings and visions of which we would not otherwise consider ourselves capable. However, if the moment is an advertiser's moment, we are seduced into feelings and visions that are nothing but inducements, and the more sweet-sounding they are the better. It could be anything from laundry soaps that have names like daydreams (Surf, Tide, Cheer, All) to the discomfort of urinary urgency ("gotta go, gotta go, gotta go"). And, of course, it is part and parcel of the platforms of national political parties, the enlistment enticements of all the military services and the idealistic prose of college catalogues.

The rarely admitted truth about the relationship between advertising and poetry is that advertising literally scabs on poetry. It enlists poetic techniques because they are attention-getters, and attention is the advertiser's pathway to increased sales. It does not matter if the thing to be sold is a commodity or a candidate. Advertisers "capitalize" on whatever is there for the selling, and the motivation is always profit of one kind or another.

But the ultimate difference between advertising and poetry goes far beyond technique. It is rooted in the fact that the aim of advertisers is to present the wares of their clients as the clients hope they will be seen while the aim of poets is to present things as they are. This is the difference between pseudo-reality or non-reality and reality itself. This is the same difference that divides fashion photography, for example, from photo-journalism, or that separates what is called "sofa art" from the paintings of Goya, Van Gogh or Edward Hopper.

Because capitalism rests on the bedrock of profit ("Money makes money," "buy cheap and sell dear," "What is so-and-so worth..." etc.), advertising has a vested interest in perpetuating the system and its "poetic" place in that system. Nor does its influence stop with the marketing of things. It is a habit of mind. Its influence in government, for example, is rampant. Viability in political campaigns these days is invariably measured in terms of each candidate's treasure chest (with the singular exception of Russell Finegold of Wisconsin). The campaigns themselves are for the most part in the hands of advertising groups, public relations firms or "spin" specialists so that the candidates often seem like minor characters or marionettes in the competitive drama of election and governance.

The ersatz poetry of advertising overwhelms our lives today at every turn. A social critic once calculated that populations in any American city receive l0,000 onslaughts a day in which they are told, inveigled or otherwise persuaded to buy what they don't need or to desire what they are made to want. The devaluation of such currency requires that everyone have the plain honesty of Diogenes, who could even be skeptical in the face of Alexander the Great. In this effort poetry is a true ally. Unlike advertising, which is a means to a desired end, poetry is an end in itself. It supports no system, capitalistic or otherwise. It is in fact our true speech which reveals the face behind the world's masks, which makes us wonder why we all too rarely see the obvious "until someone expresses it simply," which creates for us what Robert Frost called "a momentary stay against confusion," and which, finally, safeguards, not our sales, but our souls.

2007

48

A WORLD WITH NOBODY IN IT

Everyone knows that a hand-addressed envelope invites our attention sooner than one with a printed label pasted on it. The difference is that one is manufactured (made by hand, as the original etymology suggested) and the other is machino-factured. The former is personal. The latter is impersonal. The last time I checked my mail, the impersonal outnumbered the personal ten or more to one.

This is symbolic in that more and more forces in public life have led and are still leading to the elimination of the personal: elevators operated by buttons, tickets or receipts accessed through machines, telephones answered by neutered recorded voices and so on. Even the designs of most American cities are made for "people in passing"—city streets that lead only to intersections or dead ends or cul de sacs and rarely to plazas or other public eddyings where people can actually face one another and talk. The result is that people in public tend to be defined only by their destinations—even in the strolling areas of malls which are really just walkabouts intended to facilitate gawking and purchasing. And this is all buttressed by the institution of what is called "fast food," where somebody in motion can quickly re-fuel himself with some form of McSandwich and get back into the flow.

As rueful as this is from a humanistic point of view, the emphasis on impersonality has an even more profound impact on how we learn and what we think learning is. Too many have the view that students and older learners are nothing more than consumers of information, as if information and knowledge are synonymous. Any genuine educator will tell you that information at best is but a prelude to knowledge. Information, factual or otherwise, does not become knowledge until it is related to what we already know where it can be judged to be important, less important or not important at all. Information is by definition neutral—not yet personal. Knowledge is essentially personal since it bestows insights, suggests relationships, liberates us from ignorance or bias and allows us to be intelligently decisive. Merely being well informed is not the equivalent of this. Well informed people may finish high on quiz shows, but that is no indication of wisdom or good judgment. There are many well informed but ignorant people in this world.

What are the personal or impersonal implications where it comes to our reading habits? Television and computer screens are now firmly ensconced as alternatives to books, journals and newspapers. For the sake of argument let us call those who watch screens viewers, and those who scan the printed page readers. Viewers look at screens attentively, but they somehow seem once removed for what they are watching. Readers concentrate with similar and perhaps equal attention, but as they read they often reach a point where they are in direct communion with the author, the characters in a novel, the theme of a poem or essay. I think this is because viewing is somehow more public than private, while reading is more private than public, even if it can be considered public at all. For proof, look at the facial expressions of people viewing a screen compared to people reading a printed page. Which expression seems more personal? No matter how this question is answered, there remains the news that approximately 40% of the American population is regarded as functionally illiterate anyway, and 60% of the balance (6 out of 10 people) have never read a book of any kind in their entire lifetimes. Considering these numbers, is it any surprise that city newspaper after city newspaper is shutting down or that only "best smellers" or Oprah's choices are thriving with what is left of the literate population? (No one seems prompted to ask if we are better or worse as a country for having fewer newspapers. Is New York better now than when it had both the NEW YORK TIMES and the HERALD TRIBUNE?)

The depersonalization that has overtaken our country since 2000 may not be reversed for years. After the disputed presidential election, it soon became apparent that the national vote was made irrelevant. The personal choices of thousands in south Florida were never even counted. George W. Bush was elected or selected by one Supreme Court vote, probably Judge Scalia's. (When asked about this matter in public, Scalia's pat answer is "Put it behind you.") Similarly in the disputed Ohio returns in 2004, no one but Congressman John Conyers of Detroit questioned how some 400 voters in one county were able to cast more than 4000 Republican ballots. After September 11, 2001 the further depersonalization of the country swung into full throttle with the Department of Justice demanding access to bank accounts, computer records, library loans, national and trans-oceanic telephone calls and the names of persons deemed suspicious by the Patriot Act. Matters previously considered private and personal were no longer regarded as such. Enemies were re-christened "enemy combatants" and turned into non-persons who had no legal rights and could be jailed (and tortured) indefinitely. No photographs of the coffins of the military dead were permitted, and the President attended no military funeral "because he would then have to attend them all." (This is the same President who is said to speak daily to Christ, but whether he speaks in Aramaic, English, Greek, Latin or tongues is left unspecified.) The more Bush's war is made to seem a matter of good versus evil (us versus them), the more impersonal it becomes except for the uncomfortable daily deathcount, which the public is urged to accept as bearable. As year follows year, no one even bothers to ask what right we had in the first place to invade another country (any other country, however despicable its rulers) in defiance of international and constitutional law and any other moral stricture you'd care to name. The answer from press secretary after press secretary is that "We should put that behind us," which is an impersonal dismissal of the most personal and moral question of all. Nobody lives in that world (or non-world), but that is the one that we inhabit to our shame at this moment.

How is it possible to en-enter the personal world (the only one we have, actually) and avoid the sterility of the impersonal one we are led to believe is the real world? The best place to begin, to quote Al Smith, is to "look at the record," which is another way of saying that we should look at and learn from history.

Despite all the spin and the miasma of fear that the Bush administration is so good at spawning, it has been and is becoming more readily apparent by the day that we are being governed by manipulators. Whether it is the President's inner or outer circle or neither is irrelevant. The result is that this manipulation has bred a distrust of government itself, and the accumulated effect has not only made radical changes in our social life but in our very mentalities. We go to airports as if we are heading for a dental or medical examination. We are more than casually concerned about surveillance of all kinds as our private lives are more and more invaded or threatened with invasion. We act like people who are waiting for trouble to happen, and the President regularly spurs these fears by releasing "previously undisclosed intelligence." Regrettably, we do not pit real intelligence against such "intelligence," and we drift toward the fringes of the present tense in the hope that our problems will pass as all things pass.

All of these are lethal follies, and men and women in their prime are paying for them daily with their lives and limbs. If such governmental misguidance is not enough to engender everything from disgust to outright rage, what else is needed? In the face of such mendacity and the tragedy it has created, is it possible just to look the other way and somehow hope for the best? When we saw mediocrity rewarded with the nation's highest honors, as with George Tenet and L. Paul Bremer, we looked the other way. Even when we understood that the principal beneficiaries of this war were the oil interests, the military industrial complex, the ongoing repressive policies of the Israeli government (which we have dutifully replicated down to plastic handcuffs, blindfolds and hoods in Iraq) and the so-called "religious" base of the Republican party, we looked the other way. Even when we witnessed flagrant photo-ops of the President at the various service academies or when we learned that the military dead were returned covertly to our country when they should have been publicly extolled along with their next of kin by the President himself as heroes for being asked to do the impossible, we looked the other way.

At this writing a majority of the acquiescent Democratic and Republican members of Congress have signed on to let the war continue in its present status for the summer (while the Iraqi Congress is on vacation). What else can be expected except more of the same, which means more losses of American and Iraqi lives. Surely, this is a time when contemplation should be transformed into action! But if so, how? If the usual avenues and methods of participatory government have been rendered ineffective to reflect the will and consent of the governed, is it enough to love one's country in silence while silently despising its leaders? At the moment this seems small consolation, if that. But one thing can be done. In one of his major works Camus stated that we do not know who we are until we know what we can say "no" to. Such a "no" must be said at the time when it is required and not subsequently, and it must be as irrevocable as it is deeply personal and definite From that point on the "yes" of our lives can be said to begin; we know then who we are. Theodore White once wrote that "one man plus the truth equals a majority." A majority of one is usually ignored, but a majority of one raised to the millionth power cannot be. And if the "yes" of each of those lives converts itself into significant action whose exact nature may be unknowable right now, all the power in the world will not be able to silence or thwart it. But first the "no" must be said. And meant.

2007

49

FOCUS VERSUS HOCUS POCUS

STUART HERRINGTON is a Pittsburgher who graduated from Duquesne University in 1964. He subsequently served in Vietnam as an intelligence officer involved with Operation Phoenix, which resulted in the estimated capture of 60,000 Vietcong. The author of three books and numerous articles and reports on counterespionage and interrogation, he recently retired as a much respected and decorated full colonel. Because of his distinctive record as an officer and author, Duquesne awarded him an honorary Doctor of Letters degree in 2000.

Stuart and I have remained in touch over four decades, first in student/teacher situations and later as correspondents. His involvement in government affairs has not waned. As an ex-master interrogator in Vietnam, Panama and the Middle East, he was asked to come out of retirement in 2003 and evaluate intelligence-gathering procedures in Guantanamo and Iraq. After on-site inspections in both venues, Herrington was appalled by interrogation methods being used. The photographed abuses at Abu Ghraib were but one chapter in a multitude of practices that Herrington found both morally repugnant and informatively unproductive. He filed his objections in reports to the local responsible officials and to senior intelligence officers in the Pentagon. The Iraq report called attention to failures that were negating the value of intelligence collected from prisoners and detainees. Leaked in Washington, it found its way into the WASHINGTON POST and eventually into Thomas Ricks' best-selling book FIASCO, a detailed analysis of what the war in Iraq truly has become, debacle by debacle, deathcount by deathcount.

For Herrington, as stated in his report, torture and the random and often indefinite imprisonment of Iraqis were ethically flawed policies from the start. Such practices, together with post-midnight house searches and confiscation of private property, would simply turn Iraqi and world opinion against Americans, alienating in the process the very population we were trying to win over while simultaneously inspiring a more and more lethal insurgency. In 2004 Herrington expanded on his report in an article in the SAN DIEGO UNION TRIBUNE and related it to his experience in Vietnam, where he had assisted in evacuating diplomatic and military personnel and where he was the last U. S. Army soldier helicoptered from the roof of the American Embassy in Saigon. He stated in this article that erroneous military strategy when coupled with misguided interrogation practices would eventually demoralize the troops as well as the American public, create false expectations of what a hastily trained indigenous army could achieve, allow border infiltration and the creation of sanctuaries of in-country resistance to continue, make gratuitous enemies of the Iraqi people and sacrifice allies in the name of pursuing more critical strategic priorities, i.e., the "global war on terror." He concluded by stating that the outcome of the war in Iraq, if unfavorable to America and its allies (as now seems more and more apparent) "will have global, probably catastrophic consequences." Herrington's prescience in 2004 seems to have been confirmed by what has happened since and continues to happen.

Regardless, the Bush administration proclaims that the war in Iraq was right in conception but wrong in execution. Though Herrington and I disagree on the reason for the war in the first place, he now thinks that the war was wrong both in conception and execution, which is the position taken by Marine Generals Anthony Zinni and Gregory Newbold, Brent Scowcroft and Richard Clark. Opposed to them are the stay-the-coursers. This includes politicians and ideologically inclined journalists like Charles Krauthammer, William Kristol, Rush Limbaugh, Sean Hannity and Jack Kelly. These people rarely mention the price being paid for their hauteur: a minimum of two and a maximum of four soldiers killed in Iraq each day, almost 20,000 wounded of which a third have suffered incapacitating wounds, the rising suicide and post-traumatic stress rates among soldiers and veterans and the ongoing cost of $10,000,000 an hour to keep the war going. Add to this, as Herrington claims repeatedly, the interrogations with accompanying torture sanctioned at the highest levels and justified by in-house lawyers-on-demand like Alberto Gonzalez and John Yoo, and you have a tragic fiasco indeed. The irony of this is that the war was instigated by men and women who never served in the military, even during the war in Vietnam in which they ardently believed. This includes the oft deferred Vice President, Paul Wolfowitz, Douglas Feith, Richard Perle, Elliott Abrams and the like. And what of the President himself, whose murky time with the National Guard—except for the curious leave he was granted to work on the Blount campaign in Alabama—was spent defending Texas from Oklahoma.

Perhaps it is past time when President Bush and his supporters in and out of government should put their trust in men like Stuart Herrington, who know from actual experience what they are talking about. When the Army War College itself is now among those opposed to what the President proclaims is a winning policy, it surely must inject at least an ounce of doubt into the minds of even Bush's most rabid supporters unless they choose to "cut and run" from the facts. Retreating into a hypothetical future or sliming honest dissenters is no longer an option. Senators like Santorum and Frist stand for nothing but more of the same. And the rodeo-like patriotism of the ostentatiously proud has as much of a relation to real love of country as machismo and intellectual blindness have to moral courage and vision.

Stuart Herrington saw where blind militarism led in Vietnam, and he has made it his mission in retirement to warn where the same blindness could lead now but with even more disastrous consequences. It has been said that in the kingdom of the blind, the one-eyed man is king. If one-eyed kings like Herrington are saying what is true as the facts dictate and not as ideology or belief presume them to be, we ignore them at our peril.

2008

50

THE WAR WITHIN

IT'S NOT OFTEN that a war correspondent reveals the darker consequences of military service. David Wood does just that in a new book called WHAT HAVE WE LOST: THE MORAL INJURY OF OUR LONGEST WAR. Wood, a Quaker who conscientiously objected to the Vietnam War and rendered alternative service, subsequently became a war correspondent for four decades, earning a Pulitzer for his work. It was front-line reporting from Europe, South America, Africa and the Middle East.

WHAT HAVE WE LOST concentrates on Marines and others who were permanently damaged by what they were ordered to do. A Marine named Nik was with his platoon invading Fallujah when he saw a boy with something on his hand. Because there had been reports of children being used to attack Americans in the area, he trained his rifle on the boy, hesitated, waited, thought, re-thought and then fired, killing the boy. The object in the boy's hand turned out to be a toy. On returning to the States, Nik became obsessed with what he had done, even though his orders had been to shoot anything that moved. His obedience to that order ruined the rest of his life. Another instance involved a corporal who stepped on a land mine and lost one leg. His sergeant, who came to rescue him while warning others of a second mine since the enemy often planted bombs in pairs, stepped on the second mine himself and was blown to pieces. The corporal survived but was haunted by the sergeant's death for years and still is. Finally there was an incident where a Marine stabbed an Iraqi civilian in the chest and never could forget the man's slow dying afterward.

According to Wood, incidents like these injure the surviving victims or perpetrators morally, just as war itself does, particularly wars begun by the fiat of Presidents while impotent Congresses just watch. Soldiers returning with their memories from such wars often try to find relief in drugs, alcohol or, when counseling is unavailable, delayed or ignored, in suicide. The resulting statistics, which I've verified from other sources, are shocking.

In a definitive survey of suicides of men on duty from all services, the average number of such suicides per day from the Johnson-Nixon phase of the Vietnam War to the Afghanistan-Iraq era is 22 per day. Wood suggests that the number is probably higher since the military does not include suicides after discharge. Allowing for this while including the current number of 300 suicides annually in Afghanistan and Iraq, this means that there are 8,030 verifiable military suicides every year. Repeat: 8,030 suicides.

Wood claims that suicidal impulses arise when soldiers have to reconcile what they are ordered to do with a moral code by which they had lived prior to combat. He emphasizes that war reverses the moral order completely. Murder, individual or mass, is legalized on a grand scale to insure victory, which is the Academy Award of military conflict. (The poet William Stafford, also a Quaker and a conscientious objector, claimed that all wars really have two losers.)

The effects of war on those obliged to carry out lethal orders, though deemed justifiable legally, are downplayed or dismissed. Discussing this is not involved in their military training, but Wood thinks it should be if only to prevent further psychological damage, which is sure to come, later. For example, the pilot of the plane that dropped the first atomic bomb on Hiroshima was said to have suffered severe repercussions when he learned later of the devastation and loss of life. In World War II General George Patton once slapped a convalescing hospitalized soldier and called him a coward because the man broke down when Patton visited him. Wood cities similar instances and puts the blame on those "deciders" who placed soldiers in situations where they would predictably be forced to deal with moral dilemmas afterward. And similar blame should be directed to those who, even with the best of intentions, "support the troops" and "thank them for their service." This often simply relieves them of the onus of finding out if the issues provoking the war were valid in the first place. The Nuremberg trials established once and for all that no one is obliged to obey an unjust order but added that those who do are not absolved from guilt. In the case of an illegal war a similar stipulation should certainly apply. Leaving Vietnam aside for the moment, it is a matter of record that every religious denomination (Catholic, Protestant, Orthodox, Jewish and Moslem) saw no legal basis for the invasion of Iraq. After the invasion, these same denominations were silent. Why? Did their silence not make them guilty of accepting in practice what they rightly condemned in theory? This was particularly applicable to the Catholic hierarchy. Pope John Paul II, Pope Benedict XVI and Pope Francis opposed the war in Iraq, but the American hierarchy said little if anything. They encouraged prayers for the military but avoided the moral issue altogether. The same fate has befallen military forces other than our own. In a recent book called OUR HARSH TACTICS a number of Israeli soldiers made known their protests over what they were ordered to do on the West Bank and particularly in Gaza after the last retaliation. More than 2,000 Palestinians were killed, including upwards of 600 children. This was in addition to home demolition, imprisonment of Palestinians without trial and other violent excesses of the Netanyahu government. Many Israeli soldiers involved in such morally crucifying actions ended up taking their own lives, i.e. 237 suicides in the past decade or, approximately 24 annually.

When Nixon abolished the draft and created an all-volunteer military, he actually created military employees. He simply assumed that enlistees would do what they were ordered to do because they were volunteers. (This was the same Nixon who started the faux practice of equating love of country with wearing a $2.98 flag pin in your lapel and who required his staff to view the film PATTON on a weekly basis.) Encouraging such voluntary enlistments was a stagnant economy where young men who could not find employment were ripe for recruiters' pitches. The result is that enlistees are seen as being able to provide soldiery for presidentially chosen wars indefinitely.

The Bush-Cheney-Rumsfeld-Wolfowitz-Perle cabal that approved the illegal war in Iraq assumed it had the right to change regimes of any country of its choice simply because it had the power to do so. If people died as a result (Americans and inhabitants), then that simply was the price that had to be paid. The authors of such preventive wars (deemed immoral by all theologies) were never held to account and subsequently retired and lived in affluent retirement.

David Wood has detailed the suffering and waste that has resulted from the criminal folly of these men in soul-numbing detail. Read his words and grieve.

2016

51

THE DYING LIFE OF WORDS

THE DESTINY OF WORDS is to be spoken or written. In our technocratic age, this is a diluted blessing. Words continue to be spoken but with less and less concern for *how* they are spoken. People seem only concerned with saying what they want to say rather than with the way they *ought* to say it. The written (the once handwritten) word is all too often equated only with print, either via computers or similar devices. The result of both of these ongoing forms of expression is that words—in whole or in part—are not given the attention they deserve, and language itself is diverted from its very purpose in our lives.

Consider the current state of private or public speech. All of us have had the experience of conversing with people, particularly but not exclusively teen-agers and young adults, who often divorce themselves from the conversation to consult with their cell-phones or other hand-held devices. Such devices all too often take priority, and the conversation is suspended until the person with the device finishes his business with it and permits the on-site conversation to continue. Interrupted conversation, like interrupted sleep, loses its continuity. If there are multiple interruptions of this kind, the hoped-for continuity cannot be restored just as lost sleep cannot be restored. The conversationalist with the device, like a doctor, is always on call. The interruption need not always be made by someone calling in but could be initiated by the conversationalist himself who suddenly has to spot-check his messages, verify data of one kind or another or make a call he suddenly thinks he has to make.

All too frequently one finds this kind of discontinuity when one is talking with young adults. They are forever accessing their cell-phones. One often has to insist on their putting their phones aside so that a conversation with them can actually happen.

Such stillborn conversations are standard fare these days. The result is that genuine conversations, which are rooted in listening and responding so that that the conversationalists can create the conversation as they go, are becoming the exception rather than the rule in private or public discourse. What results from this is often little more than small-talk at worst or what is politely called communication at best, which is nothing but an exchange of information. It should be remembered that information is nothing but the bottom rung of knowledge. It's where conversation starts, not where it ends. Having worked briefly with high school students and then for years with undergraduates and graduates, I can say that conversations among students and teachers are the crux of real learning. Curiosity and imagination are actuated, and this leads to further study, further conversation, further growth. I had one student in the nineteen sixties who decided to become a teacher when he learned through class conversation that his understanding of a poem by Robert Frost was simply superficial and wrong. The more he read and re-read the poem, the more did it open up for him the vistas that only poetry can open. He's a teacher of literature in Florida today and attributes his choosing to be an educator to that incorrect interpretation forty or more years ago and how it made him re-think.

This leads back to understanding why we speak or write in the first place. The answer is simple and irrefutable. We speak and write in order to express accurately and faithfully what is in our minds and hearts. In its most degenerate form it surfaced in the recent presidential catfights masquerading as debates. In its most perfect form it can become literature—the expression of felt thought. The person who listens or reads what is expressed in this way can be permanently affected and can never act as if he never had the experience. This is proof enough that language in its most perfect form results not simply in communication but in *communion*. The reader or listener becomes one with what he is reading or hearing. In a society where so much emphasis is placed on speed-reading and such, many never experience what such communion means. It simply takes more time and attention to read and absorb a poem by Shakespeare, E. E. Cummings or Robert Frost than it does to read a weather report. But for those who take or make the time to *unite* with what they are reading, the rewards are multiple.

What is the fate of the written word in our time? My grandson recently told me that cursive is no longer taught. "They say," he reported, "we don't need it." For communicating factual data, directions or home addresses, this is probably true. But for expressing personal feelings I beg to differ. With regard to condolences, love or praise, I can think of no more authentic means of expression than with handwritten words on paper. Compare, for example, someone's reaction to a handwritten love letter to the same message fleetingly conveyed in an email. The difference speaks for itself. Many years ago in Stratford-on-Avon I was shown the only existing example of Shakespeare's handwritten words and signature. The content of the letter was irrelevant; actually it was a pitch for money from a struggling playwright to a possible benefactor. It was only the handwriting itself and the signature that made it valuable. Think of what it would have been like for someone to have discovered a handwritten sonnet of Shakespeare signed by Shakespeare. Imagine for a hypothetical moment that he then chose to read that same sonnet in any one of the many printed volumes of Shakespeare's work. The words would be the same, to be sure, in print or in cursive. But which version would seem by nature more authentic? Which one would make a reader feel closer to Shakespeare?

Searching and finding the personal in our daily experiences is what it means to be human. Conversation gives that to us if we are not distracted or diverted by irrelevance. Reading something written by hand gives that to us as well if only for the fact that the handwriting itself, regardless of what is written, reminds us that a particular person wrote it. Total faith in technology is capable of blinding us to this in speech and writing, and we are the losers for it.

2016

ABOUT THE AUTHOR

SAMUEL HAZO

The author of books of poetry, fiction, essays and plays, Samuel Hazo is the founder and director of the International Poetry Forum in Pittsburgh, Pennsylvania. He is also McAnulty Distinguished Professor of English Emeritus at Duquesne University, where he taught for forty-three years. From 1950 until 1957 he served in the United States Marine Corps, enlisting as a private and completing his tour as a captain. He earned his Bachelor of Arts degree *magna cum laude* from the University of Notre Dame, a Master of Arts degree from Duquesne University and his doctorate from the University of Pittsburgh. Some of his previous works are AND THE TIME IS, LIKE A MAN GONE MAD, THEY RULE THE WORLD and SEXES: THE MARRIAGE DIALOGUES (Poetry), THIS PART OF THE WORLD (Fiction),

MANO A MANO, WATCHING FIRE, WATCHING RAIN and TELL IT TO THE MARINES (Drama), THE STROKE OF A PEN (Essays) and THE PITTSBURGH THAT STAYS WITHIN YOU (Memoir). His translations include Denis de Rougemont's THE GROWL OF DEEPER WATERS, Nadia Tueni's LEBANON: TWENTY POEMS FOR ONE LOVE and Adonis' THE PAGES OF DAY AND NIGHT. In 2003 a selective collection of his poems, JUST ONCE, received the Maurice English Poetry Award. He has been awarded twelve honorary doctorates. He was honored with the Griffin Award for Creative Writing from the University of Notre Dame, his alma mater, and was chosen to receive his tenth honorary doctorate from the university in 2008. A National Book Award finalist, he was named Pennsylvania's first State Poet by Governor Robert Casey in 1993, and he served until 2003. He is currently Poet-in-Residence at La Roche College.

WA